The Sovereign Professional's Almanac

The Sovereign Professional's Almanac

Notes on Reclaiming Your Humanity at Work and in Life

ANGELA HAN

Ramses House Publishing LLC
Baltimore, MD

The Sovereign Professional's Almanac: Notes on Reclaiming Your Humanity at Work and in Life

Published by Ramses House Publishing LLC, Baltimore, MD, www.publishingforlawyers.com

First Printing, 2023
ISBN 979-8-9855653-2-4 paperback
ISBN 979-8-9855653-3-1 eBook

Notice: The book offers advice and inspiration on mental health and wellbeing to professionals.

Printed and bound in the United States of America

DISCLAIMER: The opinions expressed herein are solely the author's opinions and are based on the author's personal experience.

For everyone who feels
they've been robbed of their spirit.

And for my kids who will inevitably feel this way
as they venture out into the world.

I dedicate this to you
with the hope that you never forget who you really are.

CONTENTS

Dedication v

About the Author xiii

Preface: My promise to you...xv

Whom this is for 1

Emotions...3

Questions to ponder 5

The professional...7

High performance 9

Why I really left my job 11

New thoughts for confidence 13

"Thoughts are useless"... 15

Thoughts are useless 17

Disorganized? 19

How to get people to like you 21

When people don't like you...23

How to change your brain chemistry 25

How to deal with disapproval.......................................27

Feeling alive 29

When you need to make money 31

Are you qualified? 33

Finding love 35

Privilege 37

Privilege, pt. 2 39

Why I am obsessed with talking about privilege 41

How not to be offended 43

Honoring your sovereignty 45

When to quit 49

Managing the "hard" 51

Remember who you are 55

Resources at your disposal 57

You are the main character 59

Playing the main character 61

Enforcing boundaries 63

Having difficult conversations 65

Catastrophizing 67

Handling disappointment 71

We are all hypocrites 73

Hypocrisy vs. bigotry 75

One-dimensional statements 77

What is perfectionism? 79

Removing the shame from perfectionism 81

"The 'right' reasons" 83

What is your purpose? 85

Unpopular opinion 87

Patience 89

Other people's opinions 91

Maturity 93

The right next step 95

How to define mistakes 97

Nervous system regulation 99

We are self-centered 103

Pedestal 105

Congruence 107

Courage 109

Discipline 111

Don't feel better 113

The truth about love...115

Apologies 117

Activism 119

Toxic capitalism 121

Who is your current emotion? 123

You are a mystery, not a problem...125

Words 127

So, you want to change 129

Have your own back...131

Ancestors...133

Extremes...135

How to find the answer from within..137

Why you don't have an answer 139

Developing certainty 141

You are not overthinking 143

How to use the shitty feelings 145

How to allow feelings 147

You are not procrastinating 149

Before and after...151

Are you turned on? 153

Standard of behavior 155

The good girl living inside of you.......................................157

The function of the good girl 159

Coaching and therapy are only a fraction of the work 161

Your feelings are not a sin...165

The more darkness, the better..167

Imagination 169

"Don't compare yourself to other people"...........................173

Paradox..175

Parents 177

You are not too much..179

Everything is a tool 181

Boredom...183

Logical vs. magical..185

Why we worry 187

Ignorance... 189

The horse and the unicorn 191

Creativity 193

Sustainability..195

You are not missing anything...197

I should have 199

"I don't know" 201

How to never meet your goals 203

Admit your racism...205

Emotional labor 207

"The 'best' and the 'brightest'"..209

Question of the day ... and every day....................................... 211

How to love yourself.. 213

Everything is an illusion 215

How to feel safe while taking a risk... 217

My anger.. 219

Resentment... 221

Impossible to fail... 225

Are you broken?..227

Enough shame 229

Rest vs. productivity 231

Definition of rest... 233

When it's hard to rest 235

What is real?...237

The truth about compassion.. 239

Infinite opportunities 241

High-quality sex.. 243

What "high-quality" sex really is about 245

The real reason for consistency.. 247

"I think"...249

The truth about my marriage 251

"Why isn't it working?"... 255

Why we feel overwhelmed 257

Being an Asian woman... 259

Burning those bridges 261

My greatest shame 263

How to trust yourself 265

ABOUT THE AUTHOR

Hi, I'm Angela Han. I was a practicing lawyer for a few years before I quit in September 2022. I've been a life coach since March 2021.

Recently, I changed my title to Anger Coach and then to Sovereignty Practitioner. I help my clients practice trusting themselves completely.

Anyway, I am Korean American, and I love high-quality sex.

I don't listen to my mother. My children don't listen to me, either.

I wrote this book in part because I wanted to be famous and, in part, because the words kept jumping out of me onto the page without my consent.

I was diagnosed with OCD and bipolar 2 disorder in January 2023, but I've had symptoms for as long as I can remember.

You can blame all of my shit on my mental health condition. Just don't do that to other people, though. It's fucking rude.

My promise to you

I promise to never tell you to go against who you are. I won't even tell you to stop oversharing or people pleasing or whatever you think is "bad" about who you are. What is true to you at this moment is the exact information you need.

I will guide you on how to excavate that information so that it feels like home in your own body.

However, commitments are imperfect. I will contradict myself because humans are hypocrites. I cannot be consistently logical and principled across every instance in my life. That sounds robotic, and I am not a robot.

And sometimes, you will get some repetition of similar ideas to see how different sentences land.

When you get conflicting or repetitive information from me, ask yourself which parts of it are relevant and how each information feels for you in your body.

Which sentences evoke an explosion of magic and wonder in your body, whatever that looks like for you?

And even if you don't get full body responses to all these sentences, what if you trusted that you will get exactly what you need throughout your experience with this book?

I trust you. Do you?

P.S.: There will be portions of this book that may be triggering, depending on where you are and who you are.

I cannot promise to be a safe space for you in a world that is deeply unsafe. But as one of my mentors, Camille Leak, says, this will be a brave space.

This book will require you to be brave.

Whom this is for

An almanac has traditionally been a "manual" containing important dates, charts, and events that are relevant to a particular group of people. A more general definition of an almanac is a handbook containing information of a general interest.

This book is a collection of notes with information specifically for the sovereign professional, someone who works on their own terms dictated solely by their unique brilliance, including all the mess we've been taught to be ashamed of. I encourage you to choose only the parts that are important to you—the parts that remind you of your sovereignty and power—and discard the rest.

This is for people who have a knowing about who they are, what they want to do, where they are going ... but they have been brainwashed to believe that their knowing is false.

The nudging that you get, the drops of intuition that hit you out of nowhere: they are magical fairy dust. This anthology is to activate that fairy dust so the knowing that you have in your mind can fully drop into your body.

Because something happens when you are no longer bombarded by all the accusations that you are wrong.

You come back alive.

Emotions

In a world where emotions have been demonized and emotional experiences have been shamed, it is an act of courage to experience those emotions.

As you continue to meet yourself in these vulnerable moments and throughout this book, may you direct yourself to seeing how your emotions are the most valuable parts of your humanity to be experienced.

Questions to ponder

For the ideas and questions that resonate with you throughout this book, there is a good chance you will think "there is a lot of work to do" and that "the work feels hard."

If you find yourself in this place, know this: you are in the right place.

When something is hard, it means your brain chemistry is in action, you are creating new neural pathways. If this were easy, it would mean that you are traveling along the same old neural pathways.

Here are some questions to ponder:

1. What is something that I want to hide about myself? Am I in the mood for treating it like an exquisite gem to be protected at all costs, or am I in the mood to really share this with someone? What would I do if there were no right answer?

2. What about myself have I been taught to be ashamed of but am actually turned on by?

3. If you had full permission to be the most selfish person in the world, where would you go today?

Feel free to go as far out there as you'd like. Because imagination is the seed of reality.

The professional

A professional is someone who creates results.

Have you created results for your client or employer?

You are a professional.

The end.

High performance

What the fuck is high performance?

Why are you performing?

For whose benefit are you performing?

Your work shouldn't feel like a circus because you are not a circus animal.

Why I really left my job

I left my "dream job" of in-house counsel after almost four years.

I left because even if it met every standard I had about the perfect job, I came to see that I had low standards for myself.

We have been taught that being a corporate professional is supposed to be stressful and toxic, but the standard of a "dream job" is that it should be neither of those things.

My dream job met that standard because I subscribed to the low standards that existed for the benefit of corporate America.

When I saw this, I could not imagine continuously allowing myself to stoop to that standard. I started creating my own standards, and they were of the highest level. Not because they are better than others' standards but because they are the standards that honor who I am.

And I had the privilege and resources to take care of myself and pursue that.

The question is NOT "when will you quit your job?" Because we don't prescribe external action as the antidote to an internal problem.

The questions are:

1. What are your standards, and do you like them?
2. If you don't like your standards, how will you redefine them?
3. Once you set your own standards, what resources and privileges do you have to make them a reality?

If every bit of your desires was realistic, how would you respond to these questions?

New thoughts for confidence

Pick one thought in your mind you find intrusive, abusive, and unhelpful. Turn them around, kind of like the following:

Instead of: What if I was too rigid?
Try this: What if I was firm?

Instead of: What if I was not very effective in that meeting?
Try this: What if I did what I could with what I had?

Instead of: What if I am too proud?
Try this: What if I know who I am and what I'm capable of?

If you're worried about causing harm by being unaware of your flaws, is that really your voice talking or is it someone else's? Perhaps you have been conditioned to believe that keeping yourself small is the best and safest option for self-preservation because there is nothing more offensive to tradition than a human being unapologetically standing up for the truth.

And if you are having trouble really digesting your new thought, evaluate your new thought with curiosity. Here are some guiding questions:

- If I were to play a scavenger hunt with words, what words would I use to describe the thought I want to have?
- What evidence do I have to support this thought?

"Thoughts are useless"

Nothing is useless. Anything is useful to the extent you make it.

You decided that your law degree was going to be useful. That influenced your decision to complete the requirements to get your degree.

Your thoughts drive your decisions. When it comes to choosing your thoughts, your role is to act like royalty. Why?

Because (1) royalty doesn't just accept anything, and (2) you are royalty.

Thoughts are useless

There will be times when your thoughts *are* useless. Like when you are grieving, the last thing you need are nice, empowering thoughts that feel impossible to digest.

Thoughts are for the brain, and the brain is only one portion of the body. We have kidneys. Small intestines. Appendages.

They might not process thoughts, but they still communicate with you. Like a thumping heart or a pang in the stomach, your job is to learn their language and listen carefully.

Sometimes, your body will be unreasonable and illogical.
The impossible comes not from logic but from your illogical intuition. This is how businesses are built. How relationships are forged. How compelling decisions are made. It is basically the foundation of all things magical on planet Earth.

Here's the question: Are you going to be the magical part of this planet, or are you going to be the logical part of it?

I am already getting goosebumps for you.

Disorganized?

My book is disorganized. There is no rhyme or reason to it. But it still makes sense. You do not need to be organized to make sense.

You, exactly as you are, make sense.

If you were to believe in your soul that every part of you makes sense, which part of your soul would you lean closely into for its wisdom?

How to get people to like you

The way to get people to like you is not flattery; nor is it self-deprecation.

It is not being over-kind or playing hard to get.

It is the awareness of truth.

People don't like you because you're funny. They like you because you are telling the truth.

People don't like you because you're humble. They like you because you know the truth—that no one is better than anyone else.

People don't like you because you apologize. They like you because you are admitting an uncomfortable truth.

People don't like you because you work hard. They like you because you help people see their truth by living yours.

Be in a state of everlasting search for the truth. Practice expressing it on your own terms.

People will obsess over you without consent.

When people don't like you

Let me tell you a secret: There is a perverse, slutty, and nasty part of me that craves being disliked, misunderstood, and ignored.

It brings out the part of me that wants to defend, protect, and speak up. When I do, it gives me an opportunity to witness the part of me that is insecure.

It is an opportunity to love the part of myself that I've been told to hate about myself.

That feels so ... subversive.

But it's great because I am here to subvert the false hierarchies that keep us caged and keep us hating the parts of ourselves that deserve to be loved.

P.S.: Do you notice how every revolution in history was led by angry, subversive people? I don't know who the fuck installed the idea in our brains that anger is an inferior feeling.

How to change your brain chemistry

Trauma changes your brain chemistry because the shock hurts. So, we avoid it.

What if there was an experience that changed our brain chemistry because the shock pleasures?

Kind of like orgasms.

I don't know about you, but I don't avoid orgasms. I look for more of them.

What feels orgasmic to you right now? Go do it; and shock your brain with delight.

Change your brain chemistry.

Live to find pleasure, not to avoid hurt.

How to deal with disapproval

No matter how enlightened you are, disapproval of any kind will hurt.

It hurts because there is a part of you, sometimes big and sometimes small, that agrees with the disapproval.

It is hard to erase disapproval within yourself because your body is the only body on the planet that has experienced every rejection, criticism, and shame in your life.

Disapproval is a character that is alive and well in your own body.

It also has an evolutionary function of protecting you from the hurt, whether it is a mean comment or a bear attack. They both are threats to the body, and disapproval of threats keeps you safe.

So, honor your disappointment, your sadness, your despondence. She is there to keep you alive.

How do you honor it?

By asking yourself what makes you feel alive. That is what she's here for. Your uncomfortable feelings are here to protect you from the threat so you can stay alive.

Feeling alive

The way we experience the world around us is through our six senses—the five senses plus the spirit/gut/vibe that is undeniable but also unquantifiable.

Sometimes it's the thumping of the heart.

Sometimes, it's the goosebumps.

Use your five senses to create the experience you desire from your sixth sense.

- What smell triggers your excitement?
- What image triggers your wildness?
- Whose hand do you want to hold?
- What taste connects your mind to the heart?
- What sound awakens your genius?

Play with these questions. Come up with your own questions.

Stop looking for the right answer.

You will know when you sense what your sixth sense was looking for.

Trust her.

When you need to make money

You don't need to make anything.

Do you *need* all the money you already have? If you gave away $5.00 right now, are you going to die?

If you were to lose everything right now, what would you do? You will handle it.

It may be painful as fuck, but you will handle it.

"Need" is an illusion that keeps you indulging in undermining your ability to handle anything.

For one hot second, stop worrying about the technicalities of needing money to put food on the table.

Entertain the idea that you don't need to be, do, or have anything because you can handle anything on the fucking planet.

How does that feel?

If you can handle yourself at your worst, you can handle creating extraordinary results for your people and building your wealth.

Now go make that money because you can, not because you need to.

Are you qualified?

Are you qualified to be a professional?

Are you qualified to be a parent?

Are you qualified to speak and teach?

If you are, how do you know?

If you are not, how do you know?

Qualifications are a construct to keep some people in and keep some people out.

There is no one on the planet who is qualified to tell you whether you are qualified.

You get to decide that.

You get to decide that you are qualified to talk about "skydiving for beginners" after skydiving once because you know what it's like to be a beginner.

You get to decide that you are not qualified to perform knee surgery because there is not one thing you know about scalpels.

If you trusted yourself to be right about your qualifications, how would you decide?

Then come up with your own reasons as to why.

I decided that I am qualified to write a book because I don't need to be qualified to write a book.

There is no construct that will stop me from making my own decisions.

Don't buy into constructs that are designed to keep you small.

Finding love

People love to say that when they become parents, they will have found complete love.

I don't know if there is such a thing.

Here is a thought I've had for a very long time: "I don't know how to love. I am heartless."

So I have been on a quest to do everything I can to arrive at a place where I am confident in my ability to love.

I learned about love. I wrote about love. I decided on love. I read about love. Everything.

I am still struggling to believe in my ability to love. That is why the tireless pursuit continues.

That tireless pursuit is what allowed me to articulate love in ways other people never thought, and that is how I was able to teach myself and others how to love.

Take it from someone whose greatest struggle has been love itself:

You don't need to know how to love.

You don't need to have children to know how to love.

You don't need anything.

You ARE love—your very existence. That's it.

There is nothing to find because you already have it.

Privilege

When we do not fully appreciate and recognize the privilege of being human; we tend to resort to debasing ourselves.

We inflict pain on ourselves and others because we ignore the privilege to breathe, the privilege to have a body, the privilege to live.

When we ignore our privileges, we step into constant want and lack.

We hide because we think other people will judge—ignoring the privilege to speak.

We don't try because we are afraid to fail—ignoring the privilege to learn.

We pretend because we are afraid of rejection—ignoring the privilege of being one in eight billion.

When you ignore your privilege, you increase your chances of losing it. Because if you pretend that you don't have it, does it even matter whether you have it?

Understand your privilege. The privileges that come with your humanity, your degree, your skin color, your residence, your ability to think.

What are you doing with your privileges to sustain humanity on this planet?

Whether that is writing an apology, finally applying to that job, or hiring help, find a way to honor your humanity in its fullness every chance you get.

And be willing to do it imperfectly because the ability to show up imperfectly is also a privilege.

Privilege, pt. 2

Every time you feel like you were handed the short end of the stick, ask yourself: Where am I ignoring my privilege?

What kind of privilege do you have to be able to navigate this situation in a way others can't?

How will you use that privilege?

It is really difficult to ask these questions because you worked hard to get here, and to believe you are privileged might feel like you are disregarding your efforts. But effort and privilege can coexist. The human experience is excruciatingly unpredictable, painful, and joyful all at the same time.

We need effort AND privilege in order to navigate through these waters.

The more quickly you recognize your privilege, the more effective you will be at guiding your efforts.

Why I am obsessed with talking about privilege

I am obsessed with privilege because I am so mad at myself for not having recognized my own privilege for so long, and I feel so dumb about it.

Basically, I am projecting onto other people my own insecurities.

But is that the worst thing?

Our insecurities are part of our humanity, and they inform what we care about.

Your insecurities aren't dumb. It's information that you've been trained to process as dumb.

How not to be offended

If you're just like anybody else, you may have felt offended by what someone said in a public setting.

The thought process might have looked something like this: "How can someone say something like this? It's not right. I am so annoyed because I can't change them, but I can speak up about it. Let me tell this person how wrong they are."

Or maybe you were offended quietly on your own.

Being offended is not a bad thing. It only becomes a problem when it starts to keep you small—meaning it starts to make you feel that the person who offended you is more right than you are.

Let's say a kid argued, "The sky is purple!" You just laugh it off because the kid's opinion has no authority over your own. You know that the sky is not purple unless some galactic event is happening.

You are so secure in knowing that the sky is typically blue that someone else saying something inconsistent with your knowing is inconsequential to you.

Apply the same logic to everything you are offended by.

Why are you giving this person and their opinion authority over yours?

You may be thinking, "Well, this person has a platform, and they should not be spewing untruths like that. They need to be speaking more accurately and properly."

The underlying thought is: "Because others listening to this person will be easily influenced."

You are not trusting others to have their own agency in being able to choose their own opinions and experience the world on their terms.

You will not be able to change the way they see the world— especially if you are coming from a place where you are undermining their ability to create their own world. You are starting from a place of looking down at their capacity.

So examine the way you form and express your own opinions. Trust your own sovereignty.

As you increase your trust, you will find it easier to trust others' sovereignty because it is the hardest to trust your own.

Honoring your sovereignty

Sovereignty is your authority to govern yourself.

Imagine the laws of Canada being applicable in Argentina. It just doesn't work like that. Many countries have similar laws and similar processes, but you cannot be tried under Argentinian law in Canadian courts. That would create pandemonium.

When you experience pandemonium within yourself, chances are, you are putting yourself under trial for the standards that were never yours to begin with.

This is injustice.

How do some of these "laws" sound to you?

- "If you are a woman, it is harder to get ahead in life."
- "If you want to get ahead in life, you must graduate from college."

- "If you want to be impressive, you must make a lot of money."

Some of these sentences might feel like home. Maybe none of these sentences feels like home. Some might feel like home now but might change later. Only you would know.

But if these sentences feel like foreign policy to you, turn it upside down. For example:

"If you are a woman, it is harder to get ahead in life."

How about: "If you are a woman, you are already ahead in life."

The original sentence implies a particular definition of "ahead" that I do not subscribe to. In the revision, I get to decide what "ahead" means.

I get to decide what "ahead" means because I have also decided that I am terrible at the patriarchy and yet I am excellent at
Angela-archy.

When I lose people, I am not losing them. I am cutting out toxins. When that feels hard, it is hard because I have been conditioned to believe that other people have power over me.

When you are in your full sovereignty, no one has power over you.

When you do scary things, you dismantle false hierarchies.

When you step into your sovereignty, you are making the world a more equitable place.

In my world, I rule.

When to quit

Before this book, I wrote about 50,000+ words for another book. I thought that was going to be my book, but I was struggling because I simply could not move forward with it. Everything changed when my good friend and peer coach, Suzanne Culberg, gave me two bits of conflicting advice:

- It is easier to give birth than raise the dead.
- Is it truly a piece of shit, or is it perfectionism?

She then asked me: which sentence feels more right in your body?

The answer appeared within minutes. I could not wait to write another book that was more in line with my style. My body began fluttering with excitement. In the previous book, I was trying to be super organized with big paragraphs and chapters like a fucking graduate thesis. It was not me.

It dawned on me: I was avoiding the path of least resistance in pursuit of the impossible. I was trying to raise the dead with my previous draft of the book.

Are you allowing yourself to be wrapped up in the struggle, or is there another path of lesser resistance?

The answer does not have to appear right away. Let's invite curiosity and see what happens.

P.S.: It's okay if this feels hard. We have been programmed to believe that life needs to be hard at every corner. Life is hard—just not at every goddamn corner.

Managing the "hard"

Many times, we gravitate toward challenges: go for competitive jobs, seek inaccessible people, build businesses.

I'll admit, there are times when I was obsessive about completing something "successfully," that I thought compulsion and attachment were the only way.

And listen, if that is the way that feels true to you at the moment, why the fuck not?

I take great pleasure in watching myself get obsessive about certain things. There is a certain thrill to it. Kind of like all these diet trends, like keto and "75 Hard" and intermittent, that help you structure your "hard." For some people it works, and for some people it doesn't. It's even harmful sometimes.

But if obsessing over your success feels like sacrificing your humanity at the altar, you can still get the results you want without taking that route.

That is the first thing to know. All these die-hard "sacrificionados" have made it easy to believe that obsession and extreme commitment are the only ways to get what you want, so it also becomes easy to not try at all.

You may think, "Why try at all? Something is wrong with me."

Hard no.

It's kind of like being a lion watching ten monkeys climb up a tree and telling itself, "I cannot climb a tree like a monkey. Something is wrong with me."

Nope. The only truth here is that you watched a bunch of monkeys do their thing. The only remaining work is to find your thing.

For example, if someone you are interested in is stringing you along or you feel you are being disrespected, that person is not the partner you are looking for.

Be the lion. Roar and be loud in your natural habitat. That is the only way to find other lions.

Same thing with career and business. If you are applying for jobs, funding, or new clients, those who want something different than you will continue wanting something different than you even if they say yes to you. You will end up having to perform as a monkey when you are really a lion. That is when you will have created a cage for yourself.

Keep roaring and find other lions who find you magnificent as they are.

The reason all of this makes sense but feels hard is that you are used to being in a cage. You are used to letting other people whip you into a cage or you're creating the cage yourself based on others' standards.

This is hard. You are trying to move away from what you're used to. It's kind of like moving from a zoo animal to an actual wild animal in the safari where nobody has any authority over you. It's really, really hard.

If you had a choice, does it feel worse to stay where you are or uncage yourself into the wild?

Perhaps we always had more choice than we believed, and we just needed to hear that from a fellow lion.

Hi, fellow lion here. There are no zookeepers. You are safe to leave.

Get out there and roar.

Remember who you are

Releasing yourself into the wild is terrifying because you never had to hunt, catch, and kill on your own. It is very possible that you may get hurt in the process. Remember: you belong in the wild. You already know at the soul level how to hunt, catch, and kill.

Find your pack. Find the people who are masters at thriving as they are.

Learn how to hunt, catch, and kill.

Except you are not really learning. You are remembering who you really are.

Resources at your disposal

When you free yourself into the wild (aka your own sovereignty), notice the vast and endless land filled with resources at your disposal.

See them. If you are so focused on your inability to hunt like the lions that have been in the wild for decades ahead of you, you will never see the resources.

When you get a random check in the mail, notice it. Accept it. Acknowledge it. Appreciate it.

When you get a compliment, when you get a call from your family. Same thing.

Receive all the love, resources, and power available to you. That is the only way to use them to your advantage.

You are the main character

Have you ever run in the rain or sat in a nice coffee shop thinking that you are the main character of a movie, and then suddenly feeling ashamed of thinking that about yourself?

But what about the actors who play the main characters in movies? What makes them so special? They are there because they got comfortable with the idea that it is possible to be the main character in a movie.

Consider this: Let's say you are capable of glamorizing everything that you are doing. Writing in your PJs. Thinking while picking your nose. Cleaning up the can of tomato soup you spilled all over the kitchen floor. All of it.

Truly imagine strutting on as glamorous as you'd like, whatever glamor feels like to you. Maybe regal is your word. Maybe magical. Maybe royal.

You are the main character.

Imagine for a minute longer than you feel comfortable: what does that look like? Feel like?

Psssst, when you are doing this, you are rewiring your brain to believe that you are the main character and that you are unfuckwithable.

Playing the main character

Why does it feel so awkward to imagine myself as a main character?

Because you have been brainwashed by generations before you who believed they cannot be the main character.

Because you have been told by authority figures that you cannot be the main character.

Because you have been told by peers and those whose thoughts you value that you cannot be the main character.

So we look for evidence that what they say is true. So we become the loudest voices that believe we cannot be the main character.

Surround yourself with those who believe you are the main event. Because you are. It is your life. There is no other main character in your life.

Brainwash yourself with the idea that you are the main fucking thing; and start living life on your own terms.

Enforcing boundaries

When people violate my boundaries, I do not always confront them about it directly.

The reason is there is a very high chance that they will ask me to explain myself, which I am not available for because that is what I call free emotional labor.

Free emotional labor is when I facilitate their getting what they want, which is to be part of my world or to be heard by me to increase their sense of belonging.

I am not responsible for their sense of belonging unless we have entered into a consensual relationship where I agree to help them achieve an emotional goal.

I value my space, energy, and expertise. When I constantly communicate on my own terms that I am in search of only those who honor me and my skills, those who feel entitled to it will slowly transition out of my space. I am left only with those who treat me with the highest level of respect.

That is why I find it valuable to be in constant connection with myself so that I do not require others to perform any emotional labor on my behalf.

We all deserve the highest level of respect.

Having difficult conversations

We don't typically like difficult conversations. We may even avoid them for long stretches of time.

There could be myriad reasons, perhaps including, but not limited to, the following:

- You and your thoughts might get rejected.
- The rejection might not be outright; it might be slow and pernicious.
- You might fumble or make a mistake.

When you get rejected or feel like you did not do something the right way, you may think you don't belong. When you think you don't belong, it is difficult to find purpose behind the difficult conversation. "It's just not worth it," we think.

Here are my questions: What IS worth fighting for at the expense of feeling like you belong?

What is the hill you are willing to die on?

Whenever we start something, quit something, say something, we always risk being booted out by other people. We also risk being accepted by people we didn't even know existed. Think about the times people supported you at your worst. For them, you are worth fighting for.

If you have to tiptoe your way around people, and you constantly feel like you don't belong, they are the ones who are not worth being around.

The reason you may feel like this is unrealistic and selfish; you have been programmed to believe that being surrounded by people you deserve is "too good to be true." Start entertaining the idea that it is not too good to be true.

Every time you have a difficult conversation and are willing to feel uncomfortable asking for what you desire, you get one step closer to what you deserve. Because even if you get rejected, you will just have eliminated a circumstance that does not deserve you.

Catastrophizing

Catastrophizing starts with the phrase "what if."

What if I don't get what I want?

What if not getting what I want makes other people think less of me?

What if other people thinking less of me leaves me out in the streets?

I would do this regularly during arguments in my marriage. I would mentally tally up the number of times we argued, and I would try to aim for no more than once a month. If we argue more than once a month, then our marriage would be going in the wrong direction. That was my belief.

I made up all these rules about marriage all on my own. And whenever I did not measure up to these self-imposed standards, I would catastrophize the situation:

- What if we fight more than once a month?

- What if fighting more than once a month means I am a bad, ineffective person?
- What if being a bad, ineffective person means my husband will leave me, and I will be left on my own? Better start planning for that divorce.

And then I would show up expecting to get into a fight, pushing myself to the edge, looking for fights, seeing how much I can push our marriage so that we can deal with the worst of ourselves.

I was trying to make the perceived catastrophe happen in real life.

This was a classic trauma response from my parents' divorce. I processed the divorce as an end result of the constant arguments between my parents, so my trauma response was trying to rip the bandage off by having as many arguments as possible so that I wouldn't be surprised by the end result. So that I would be right.

Wanting to be right is an evolutionary response because being wrong could kill us. If our paleolithic ancestors went to the wrong side of the hill, they could be attacked by predators.

Catastrophizing is the byproduct of trauma and evolution. It is human.

Notice your resistance to this very common feature of humanity.

Consider the reality that catastrophizing has had the function of allowing you to survive. Nothing has gone wrong.

Ask a different "what if" question: What if not getting what you want directed you to fulfilling an even greater, deeper desire?

You just might find yourself in the midst of transitioning from "catastrophizing" to "miracle-izing."

I began asking myself this question: What if my husband is showing me the parts of me I've been refusing to look at?

I began releasing the desire to be right and leaning toward the desire to be curious.

I stopped being so vigilant of arguments.

Tiny miracle-izing in action.

Handling disappointment

Every time something I don't like happens, I ask myself, "What if this saved my life?"

This doesn't mean we need to be in an eternal state of gratitude and grace. That's just weird, unrealistic, and almost inhumane.

I'm talking about having awareness of the full truth.

Yes, you may have missed out on an experience that you were really looking forward to or you may have gotten disappointed by not meeting your goals. And, at the same time, what if the fact that the canceled meeting or the disappointing experience actually saved your life?

Maybe by not going to the meeting you were able to avoid a car accident, or because of a missed revenue target, you came to a clear understanding of what is most important to you.

Now, how does it feel to have full permission to both feel the disappointment and feel the safety of where you are right now?

We are all hypocrites

In God's honest truth, can you say that you have never contradicted yourself?

Some easy examples:
- Flaking out on new year's resolutions
- Breaking marriage vows
- Not treating others the way you want to be treated

More examples are not hard to find. This is another feature of humanity because the human experience is so vast and multi-dimensional.

We have thousands of thoughts a day and make hundreds of decisions each day. It is impossible to be consistent with our values and principles across all instances.

In fact, every time we are hypocrites, we are taking quantum leaps because we are changing our minds and remaining flexible about what could be true and possible.

This does not mean we aim to be hypocritical. Instead, notice any resistance to the fact that we change our minds all the time because we are exposed to new information all the time. New information could include different moods, new ways of thinking, facts, information you see on the news, or other people's opinions that resonate with you.

In fact, when we become more comfortable with the fact that we are more hypocritical than we'd like, we become more flexible when we see hypocrisy in others.

Hypocrisy vs. bigotry

Hypocrisy is an incongruence between our thoughts and actions at different times or in different settings.

Bigotry is allowing hypocrisy only among certain groups of people on the basis of their privilege.

Hypocrisy is a feature of humanity. Bigotry is a destroyer of humanity.

One-dimensional

statements

I am not an ambassador of one-dimensional statements like:

1. Don't care about what other people think.
2. Stop being afraid to show up.
3. Stop trying to be perfect.
4. Be consistent.
5. You must enforce your boundaries.

These are instructions meant for a robot because humans are not one-dimensional. This is my reality:

1. I care about what other people think. I care about my work even more exceptionally.
2. I have fear written all over me. I am just very skilled at experiencing fear.
3. I try to be perfect all the time. It is part of my creative process, like when I try to find the perfect word when I communicate.

4. I exemplify inconsistency. My ability to change my mind speaks to how rapid my expansion is.
5. I let people cross my boundaries because I am an amorphous creature, not the fucking DMZ.

Caring about people's opinions, fear, perfectionism, inconsistency, messy boundaries: these are features of life. There is no universe where life exists without them. To get rid of them is to erase our humanity.

The point of all these experiences is to know how to use them, not delete them. Kind of like riding the wave, not avoiding the wave. Riding them is way more enchanting.

Challenges don't exist to be overcome. They exist to be transmuted into your own magical scepter.

Where in your life are you trying to box yourself into a one-dimensional statement?

What is perfectionism?

I have no idea.

But I know what perfection is. It is a decision.

I am perfect because I decided.

Perfectionism is something that happens when we struggle to make that decision.

Sometimes, life is all about telling perfectionism to fuck off because I am already perfect.

Removing the shame
from perfectionism

While we dismantle perfectionism, we must also know that there is also no universe where perfectionism does not exist.

Which means to shame perfectionism is to deny our humanity. And it is fruitless. It's kind of like shaming the Earth for having water.

When your perfectionism shows up, notice the way it is simply a manifestation of your humanity:

- You care deeply about the work you do when you are trying to meet your deadlines.
- You care deeply about the people you work with because you can relate to their basic emotions.
- You care deeply about expanding your capacity while trying to improve your way to higher quality work.

Your perfectionism is beautiful. It is a feature of your vastness.

When you arrive at the moment that perfectionism becomes so overwhelming that it pushes you to depart from your vastness, that is when you disengage.

Kind of like water—the perfect amount will be soul quenching, but too much of it will drown you.

Play and explore with perfectionism and discover where YOUR boundaries are with your own perfectionism.

"The 'right' reasons"

Fuck the "right" reasons. Who are the "right reason" police? Why do you need to have the "right" reasons? What the hell is the "right" reason?

Stop worrying about whether you got it right or wrong. Because you are so much bigger than the binary of "right" and "wrong." Meaning: whatever you do, someone will think you are wrong, and someone will think you are right.

It is exhausting to follow anybody else's definition of right or wrong when it leads you outside of your own knowing.

The real question is: If there was no such thing as right or wrong, what would YOU desire to do?

Sometimes, your body knows before your brain and acts before you can catch up. Kind of like the way we feel chemistry with someone for no logical reason. You might not sense chemistry with everything you do, but when you sense it, keep following it.

Even if you mess up, it just means you're in the middle of experimenting. You're tightening your relationship with your body's signals. You're fine-tuning the antennas that guide you through the world.

You'll never arrive at right or wrong.

Instead, you'll arrive at your truth.

What is your purpose?

I always felt off whenever someone said, "Your purpose is to serve others." For a while, I thought I was the weird and wrong one.

But whenever you think you are weird and wrong, there is an intelligence waiting to be seen.

The idea of serving others as the priority felt off to me for a reason. The reason was that it was just not true for me.

What was true for me instead was that my purpose was to express myself. I am on this planet to be expressed. Kind of like a piece of artwork. Or a math equation.

So, here's my question: how do you want to express yourself today?

P.S.: Shoutout to one of my teachers, David Bedrick, for inspiring this chapter.

Unpopular opinion

There is no such thing as an unpopular or popular opinion.

Whatever you say will make you unpopular somewhere and popular somewhere. When you preface your opinions with "unpopular opinion," you start with the attention of those who will find your opinion unpopular.

Just speak. The rest will follow.

Patience

Patience is just the willingness to be impatient.

If you are being impatient right now, you are also being patient; as long as you don't die from impatience, you are allowing impatience.

You, patient one, you.

Other people's opinions

If you are feeling the jitters because it might piss people off, remind yourself that in a hundred years (at most), we're all going to be dead.

Might as well piss them off. They won't remember it. Especially if they're going to be dead.

And a hundred years is a long time. If I'm actually going to live that long, might as well get comfortable with the jitters because this won't be the last time I get them.

We'll get jitters for some other reason some other time, many times. That's us practicing helpful thoughts and expanding our capacity for the future. Go, us.

Maturity

Maturity is not a thing.

It's made up to make you feel like you're not doing the right thing at the right time according to other people's standards.

Maybe I am not meeting others' standards, but that has nothing to do with my maturity. Because it doesn't exist, and even if it did exist, I get to decide what is right and when it is right.

How terrible would it be if everybody was "mature?" We would have to act all serious in certain places, and that is no service to the fullness of our humanity.

May you never find the need to be mature and suffocate yourself and others with the conditioned boringness that takes the wind out of your spirit's sails.

The right next step

Sometimes we get into things by accident or on purpose.

Sometimes our brain leads. Sometimes our body leads. They are equally valuable.

Sometimes there is a reason, sometimes there is not.

You are capable of following both logic and intuition.

Sometimes there is no rhyme or timeline to it. Sometimes you have no idea.

That is why the mystery is so fun. We get to keep unpacking the mystery of the universe and the mystery of your humanity.

How to define mistakes

In whose eyes is it a mistake? If not yours, then why are they right?

Who is benefiting from calling it a mistake? If not you, then how are they using your mistake to make you smaller?

If it is still a mistake in your eyes, is it really a mistake if it made you curious about what's next?

Mistake? Not a chance.

More like a redirect.

Nervous system regulation

The nervous system gets triggered when you experience a familiar shock from a past stressful or traumatic event.

When the nervous system is triggered, it becomes dysregulated. When it becomes dysregulated, it focuses on the trigger, leaving little space for any other information for the nervous system to process.

So, when we take action from a dysregulated state, we often take action that does not truly take into account all the information that is relevant to the decision we are making.

That is why we often lash out at people around us when we act from a dysregulated state.

There are many ways to regulate the nervous system, including some of the following: taking space for yourself, connecting with someone else for support, breathing exercises, writing exercises, actual physical exercises.

When you separate yourself from the trigger to process the event, meaning, understanding your triggers, the effect it has on your body, and the effect it has on your decisions, you are able to separate your identity from the trigger so that you can create some space for additional information before you make decisions, such as how to interact with those around you.

A lot of the mental health space is dedicated towards nervous system regulation because it allows us to take action from a grounded place and a place where we are more in touch with our true emotions and desires.

It is an honorable pursuit.

At the same time, sometimes, you do not have to regulate shit. Especially if you carry an unmanageable burden of having more vulnerable spots that can be triggered. For example, a white man cannot be triggered for being discriminated against in a million different ways as a black woman would because he has never been a black woman.

We do not want to defer the responsibility of addressing our own triggers. No one is going to come rescue us from our triggers. Nor are they an excuse to go around lashing out at everybody.

But to ask those who carry an unmanageable load to be as regulated as those with a smaller load is unreasonable and inhumane.

And when we do lash out, what if we actually do have quite enough information to make the decision to lash out?

Sometimes, we are exhausted. Sometimes, that is all the information we need. Sometimes, we will cause harm. But there is no universe where the harm caused on people as a result of being non-male, non-white, and cis gendered can be outweighed by the harm we cause to claim our stake in the ground.

When we lash out, it is the soul behind the nervous system dislodging itself from an unsafe space with force because in its imperfect human capacity, it feels like it has no other choice but to lash out.

Yes, nervous system regulation is a lifelong pursuit not to be ignored. At the same time, your nervous system is only a part of you. Whatever you decide, trust that it was the result of your soul speaking its truth and disobeying the rules because it recognizes your bigness beyond rules and logic.

We are self-centered

True, we think we do more work than other people. Suffer more than other people. Are more right than other people.

But then again, that makes sense. When we think we are not as right as other people, we get our ass to work and try to get there to be better than they are.

Being self-centered lets us keep moving in the direction we want to go. If we had spent half the time doubting our self-centeredness toward trusting our self-centeredness, we would expand our capacity to trust ourselves. When we trust ourselves, we trust others, too. It's like a muscle.

Pedestal

All these people you are putting on a pedestal, you are doing that for you.

It feels comfortable to know that there is someone who knows better than you. But don't be disappointed when you discover that you have more power than they'll ever have over what is possible for you.

Use them to the extent that they offer evidence of your own power. Anything beyond that becomes mental masturbation. It's pleasurable and familiar, but you'll find yourself wanting to hide that part of yourself where you're deferring your power to someone else.

Go own your power and have an actual, powerful climax by recognizing that you own the pedestal.

Congruence

Everything you do is for yourself. Even when you are "sacrificing" your time and energy for other people, you are doing that because it somehow benefits you and your narrative about who you are.

Many times, we have bought into the story of who we are based on what others have said about what we ought to be. For example, many of us have been trained to be "good" even when we don't want to, so we do everything in our power to maintain the "good" in us even when it feels like a lie.

If everything we do is self-serving, why not do it in a way that feels the most truthful?

This is congruence. Congruence is the alignment of who we really are and what we do.

When we try to be "good" even when we don't want to, it breeds resentment and anger. When who we really are and what we do are not congruent, it also perpetuates systemic inequities.

For example, when we try to be "not racist" and deny the fact that we are all racist in some capacity, we ignore the experiences of groups without institutional power, and that is inherently racist. We are living a lie, and that creates a divide between those who experience the racist reality and those who have the privilege of living outside that reality.

Here are the two questions to ask:

1. What is the part of me that I am not 100% honest about?
2. How do I want to move closer to the 100%?

Absolve yourself from the need to be perfect right now. Root for yourself for the process. Not the end result.

Courage

Courage is not attached to a particular form of action. Showing up in front of others is not the only place you can find courage.

You can find courage in deciding to not show up for others and instead showing up for yourself. Especially in a world where you face pressure to show up where people can see you.

Before you show yourself to anyone else, see yourself first. How does courage show up when you look at yourself in the mirror?

Discipline

If you want a bit more discipline in your life:

In your world, what is the opposite of discipline? Maybe flexibility, flow, love, unevenness, neglect, disorder, ignorance. There is no right answer. Which one of these words, if at all, feels closest to the opposite of discipline?

Whatever that word is, notice if you are resisting it. Are you resisting love? Flow? Disorder?

Take that word, and ask yourself: what does it look like to allow more of it in my life?

Then watch discipline slowly come back.

For me, the opposite of discipline is un-evenness. I don't like when my habit tracker looks uneven or when my calendar becomes uneven because I think I don't have enough discipline to work out, for example.

And then I allow a bit of the unevenness. I let my habit tracker look like a haphazard chicken scratch. I allow space on my calendar for a bit of lateness and shifting around.

And when I stop demonizing the unevenness, the discipline slowly comes back. I start getting bored with the unevenness and want to make my habit tracker and calendar even again. I want to get back to working out because I want to feel even and whole again. I started coming back to discipline out of desire, not willpower.

You can use this for anything in the world. Whether it's discipline, motivation, health, respect, prestige, whatever it is that you think you are lacking, try this exact exercise and see what happens.

Don't feel better

Stop trying to make people feel better unless they specifically ask for it.

Why are we discriminating against certain feelings within the full spectrum of human emotions?

We have been so caught up prioritizing "feeling good" that we lack the skills of how to feel terrible because we are so busy avoiding them.

And why is "happy" better than "lonely" or "sad"? The most valuable emotion is whatever emotion is true at the moment.

To deny people the opportunity to sit in the darkness is insulting to the wholeness of humanity they get to experience. We all deserve to be honored where we are.

The truth about love

While we increase our capacity to love ourselves, we are unlikely to ever perfect our skillfulness at loving ourselves.

Here's what most people will not admit: we require a lot of help from other people by experiencing other people's love to feel closer to believing that we actually deserve love.

That is why we receive an ungodly amount of love from unexpected places that have nothing to do with the work you are doing to love yourself.

Because the love you deserve is unconditional.

Yes, keep working on loving yourself when you are available because it's great. Regardless of it all, you will continue to receive truckloads of love.

I hope you are available to catch it all.

Apologies

Incorrect statement: Most people are too proud to apologize.

Less incorrect statement: Many people, more often than not, have moments when they are too proud to apologize depending on their view of the situation and their life experiences, including trauma and conditioning.

Activism

Everybody is an activist in their own way. How you show up today is perpetuating something.

When you make the decision to have another vegan meal, you just move the needle towards sustainability in your own way.

When you make the decision to disregard your business because it didn't make any money today, you are perpetuating toxic capitalism where you are valuable only when you are generating money.

Don't use these statements to shame your decisions. Use these statements to inform your decisions.

What are the thoughts that are driving your actions?

And how are your actions furthering a particular concept or movement?

Who you decide to be matters to the future of this planet and civilization.

The good news is that there is no right or wrong way to be an activist. The false binary just makes us hide more out of fear of messing up.

The even better news is that right now, you get to make the decision of how you want to show up. Even the decisions that appear to be affecting just you, it is actually affecting everybody else because the way you talk to yourself will be reflected in how you talk to everybody else.

The words you choose to entertain in your mind and body are important. May you fall in love with the words you choose for yourself.

Toxic capitalism

Capitalism can be toxic because it celebrates humanity only when (1) it is in competition and (2) those in the competition win. Most times, the competition is won by making as much money as possible.

As a result, the global culture is now imbued in the need to make as much money as possible to avoid a sense of worthlessness. So there is an obsession with scaling and delegating and hustling until you've won. Except there is no such thing because there is no clear definition of winning except "having more," which feeds a constant loop of obsessing forward.

In the midst of the fast-paced movement, we forget about the community gardens. The laundry to fold. The silence in between things. We forget about the value of all those things because they don't "make us money."

That is why we, as a society, are deeply steeped in the belief that the working parent's time is more valuable than the non-working parent's time. We have collectively decided that the working parent deserves to rest at home while the stay-at-home parent continues to take care of the kids until the parents go to bed.

Another belief we have is that our business is worthless unless it is making money. Thousands of people are giving up in their businesses because they believe that the value of their business is its ability to create a profit. I have been told this many times, too.

I resist that message.

Here is how I define sustainability:

"Low revenue" months are irrelevant because my work is always working. "High revenue" months are unsurprising because my work is always working.

What sustains my business is how I approach it.

If I attach my business' value solely to money, I'll give up on my business and go back to a job at the expense of my humanity and safety.

Because I refuse to attach any part of my life to money, I am resourceful when I need resources. What kind of resources do I have the privilege of asking for? What kind of skills do I have that will be most useful right now? What can I make possible right now even without x, y, and z? With each question, I detox from the capitalistic thinking that my worth is conditional to the end result.

Unsubscribe to toxic capitalism and celebrate your humanity regardless of how much you make. If you have your back with problems that come with no money, you will have your back with problems that come with more money.

Who is your current emotion?

Notice if there is an emotion in your body. Most of the time, it is not just one emotion. It is a mixed potion of different feelings alchemizing, moving throughout your body. Do you feel it?

Name that emotion. Give it their own name. It could be Bob. Or Calientina.

When were they born? What has their journey been like? Paint a story of their life.

Notice the way you honor who you are as a holder of that emotion. Notice the alchemy of the emotions that exist in your body and keep your spirit alive.

You are a mystery, not a problem

Is it really problematic that you're not always consistent? Imagine your life partner doing the exact same thing every single day for the rest of your life together. It would feel very predictable and boring.

We are always going in different directions. Sometimes expected, sometimes unexpected. You are constantly exploring uncharted terrain because you are an ever-evolving, multi-dimensional universe. It can feel scary to explore new parts of who you are, sometimes surprised by it. Your exploration never makes you a problem.

You have been taught to believe that you need to be "good." But a mystery is bigger than "good." It is simply indescribable and beyond comprehension. So anything you experience within the mystery of who you are, it is irrelevant and fruitless to call it problematic.

If you were to explore one more layer, dimension, path, facet of the mystery that you are, what would you be thinking, feeling, and doing today?

Words

Words are often inadequate descriptors of our actual experience.

As my teacher David Bedrick says, "Your anger can be different from my anger."

When we use conventional vernacular to describe our physical and emotional experience, it often contains the vastness of our experience.

If you do feel angry, where in your body are you feeling it? Is it moving? It is hot or cold or lukewarm? Is it sparkling or is it dull? Is there a color, a smell, or a speed to it?

If you feel like words are inadequate to express how you are feeling, drop into your body. Your "anger" is bigger than the word itself. Peel back each layer one by one, and offer sensory words one by one as you answer questions like the above.

Remember, you are a mystery. This is how you discover more of yourself, one sensory experience at a time.

So, you want to change ...

I understand that you have several things you want to change about yourself. Maybe a few bad habits. Maybe you want things to look a little different in your life. Chances are, you are beating yourself up for not getting there fast enough.

Consider the thawing of meat. You can make it thaw faster when you microwave it. But the taste is going to be weird. You know that the best way to get all the juices and maximize the chances of it cooking evenly to the state of *chef's kiss* is by letting it take time to thaw.

You are doing the same thing. If you have been in a particular state of being, it takes time for you to change that state. You are thawing. You have been frozen into doing all the right things your entire life. Allow yourself to let go of doing all the "right" things just one at a time.

When you are thawing, you deserve warmth, patience, and care. How will you give that to yourself today?

Have your own back

Think about the worst-case scenario. My worst-case scenario is having to sell my house, lose my family, and be left out on the street with no car, no bank account, no phone.

Will you have your own back then?

Whatever your answer is, let's be okay with that. Nothing like, "It should be a yes." It shouldn't be anything other than what it is right now.

On a scale of 1-10, ten being an absolute yes, where are you on the scale?

Let's say you are at a 5. You cannot expect a 5th grader to get to 10th grade in an instant. But a 5th grader can ask questions about what it is like to be a 10th grader. How to get there. Some tools and strategies on making the journey manageable.

Same thing here. You can ask questions to yourself like:

What does it feel like to be at 10 with absolute certainty that I will have my own back in the worst-case scenario?

- What kind of thoughts will I have?
- What kind of decisions would I be making?
- How will I be resourceful?
- What is one thing I can think or do today that feels like a no-brainer to help me get to a 10?

Assuming you want to get to a 10 and assuming that you will inevitably get there. Just not overnight.

Once you get there, imagine all the ways you will have your back in any scenario that is not as bad as the worst-case scenario. You'll have your back so easily when you make a mistake or fart during a conference call. The journey will be so much more hilarious and awesome.

Happy trails.

P.S.: Shoutout to my coach, Simone Seol, for inspiring this chapter.

Ancestors

Every time you think to yourself "I should know how to do this by now," think about the centuries it took for our collective community to decide that women deserved to not die.

The centuries it took for black people to have a vote.

And it's STILL going on.

Every time you decide to free yourself from the oppression of your soul by noticing where you are buying into the historical narrative that you are undeserving, your ancestors are singing and dancing.

They are celebrating the way you are undoing centuries and generations of trauma, just one thought at a time.

Centuries later, how do you want to be witnessing your descendants?

Let's never give up, no matter how slow it feels. Our ancestors are celebrating, and our descendants are waiting.

Extremes

I was raised in a culture where people pleasing was the norm. We would share a lot of empty words to fill up the space and bow to elders even when we had no respect for them. I was taught to please others first before ever thinking about my own needs.

This is not to say that my culture is completely devoid of greatness. I love every part of my culture, both the great and the not-so-great because it produced me.

After being brainwashed to believe that pleasing others needs to be at the top of my priority list, I am now all about pleasing yourself first. This shows two things:

1. Even when you are brainwashed in your most formative years, your brain cannot quite be washed 100%. Even if you are force-fed sentences into your brain, your body will know differently because when the brain accepts words, the body can reject it or process it differently. So, no one can take who you really are away from you.

2. Sometimes, you need to experience extreme conditions to arrive at the opposite extreme. Because I was in a place of

extreme people pleasing, I was able to experience the extreme pain and suffering that came with people pleasing. That gave me a comprehensive set of tools to deal with people pleasing at every level, so now I can arrive at the other side of putting myself first before anything else.

Same with other concepts:
- Extreme confusion helps you arrive at extreme clarity.
- Extreme loneliness helps you arrive at profound closeness.
- Extreme pain helps you arrive at the best antidote for pain.

Because we are wired to address the challenges we are confronted with.

Extreme conditions are not always helpful. We don't need to be jumping around in extreme conditions all the time.

However, when we do find ourselves in extreme situations, we are actually very close to mining what appears to be so distant from where you are.

How to find the answer from within

Think of a question you have right now that you're really wanting an answer for.

1. Is there such a thing as a right or wrong answer to this question?

If the answer is no, then you don't really need an answer. What you really need is a decision because there is no wrong way to go about it.

If the answer is yes, then you are likely thinking about whether you are making the right decision or the wrong decision.

2. Are you willing to be wrong about it?

If you are wrong about the answer to this question, does it cause tangible harm or damage? And even if it causes tangible harm or damage, are you able to handle the consequences? (I would bet that you are able to handle anything.)

Now the question is why you should risk needing to handle the consequences, which brings us to the last question.

3. Does this answer make you feel alive?

Look at the ways your body is reacting to this answer. Perhaps your chest is pounding. Or your body feels super light in the best way. Or you suddenly need to take a shit.

Are you willing to accept these communications from the body as indicators that you are going in the right direction, even if it "seems" wrong?

If not, maybe we're just not meant to meet the answer we're looking for right now. Maybe all we need is a moment to sit with the desire for the answer.

Note: You get better at making decisions based on your aliveness as you practice feeling alive. Practice being in the state of aliveness, whatever that looks for you. Be willing to be wrong because there is no such thing.

Why you don't
have an answer

How many times has someone asked you a question that you don't know the answer to, but you answered it anyway just to keep the conversation going?

If you want to have an answer, you will find one. Even if it means making it up. Even if it is "made up," it is the product of your brain. Your brain submits the first thing that comes up. What if you trusted that?

Decide that you want an answer. Just to keep the conversation going with your own self. What is the answer you arrive at?

The reason you think you don't know the answer is that you don't want to know the answer. Because it is scary. Because there are multiple answer choices, and we don't want to pick one.

That's ok. We're just spit balling here.

Developing certainty

When we are craving certainty, it is likely because we are craving certainty for one particular outcome.

For example: "I want to be certain that my decision to take this job is the right one."

Ask yourself this question: Do I feel more powerful when I say yes, or do I feel more powerful when I say no?

Suddenly your body will communicate to you your power in unusual and interesting ways.

You are not overthinking

This is the loop of our thinking:

1. Something happens
2. I have thoughts about it
3. The thoughts make me feel bad
4. I should not feel bad

The overthinking is the repetition of 2–4. The only way to "stop the overthinking" is to eliminate 4. You have thoughts about what happened, and the thoughts make you feel bad. Allow yourself to feel bad.

We are "overthinking" because we are not allowing ourselves to think. Stop practicing brain supremacy by thinking that your brain has more information than your body.

Listen to your body. Connect with your body and notice all the ways your body is being alive and being affected by your thoughts from your brain.

That is the beginning of sitting with your feelings.

How to use the shitty feelings

We may technically know that we don't need to fix anything. But the thoughts keep coming up:

- "I need to do this better."
- "I should have done that differently."
- "That was not the best way to handle it."

Whether these statements are objectively true, the desire to fix does drive you. If you like being driven, let that desire be. Even if it is annoying.

And if you want to take a break from being so driven, let it exist then, too. Because whatever shitty feeling you are trying to resist, they will come back tenfold.

Experience the dose you have now before it comes at you like a tsunami.

How to allow feelings

What do people mean when they say "sit" in your feelings? Do you have to sit?

All that you are required to do is notice when you are trying to distract yourself from the emotion. Whether the emotion is joy or sadness or thereabouts.

Your distraction could be worrying or scrolling through Instagram.

Notice when whatever you are doing is pulling you away from the emotion.

When there are minimal distractions, you will finally be able to see the emotion more clearly because more of your brain and body is now available to feel it and engage with it.

That is all that "sitting with" and "allowing" your feelings means.

P.S.: Sometimes, it just feels easier to stay in the distraction and that's fine. It is probably because it feels so uncomfortable and painful and even traumatic to allow an emotion. It is human to distract ourselves from acute pain, kind of like the way we scream and screech when we touch a hot pan. That is a function of our survival. Allow your feelings only when you decide to be available for it.

You are not procrastinating

Procrastinating is a word invented by the self-help industry to make you feel bad about yourself.

It is not a thing.

Hunters and gatherers did not "procrastinate" because their work was simple and important: hunt and gather for survival.

If you are not doing what you think you're supposed to be doing, it likely means that it's just not as simple and as important to you. Which means it's just not worth your time, energy, or resources.

Don't make yourself wrong for not wanting certain things in life. No one deserves to be forced to want something. It doesn't work that way anyway.

Before and after

The culture of "before and after" perpetuates the scarcity mindset of wanting to be "on the other side" when there are no sides.

Even after you quit your job.

Even after you start your dream business.

Even after leaving your spouse.

Even after you "become healthier."

You will still go through dark moments afterward. It's not just love and light moving forward.

Darkness is everywhere. It's a matter of which darkness you prefer.

What kind of darkness reaches through the crevices of your soul in a way that allows you to experience and feel your humanity even when you cannot see anything?

What kind of darkness offers you the kind of depth that you may not be able to sense right away?

For example, I felt a darkness in my job because I felt the darkness was forced upon me. The darkness felt like a cave I would never get out of.

On the other hand, the darkness I feel now when there is uncertainty feels more like a mystery to be explored because I claim that darkness for myself. Kind of like the masturbation rooms at sex shops, where you can't see anything, but you know some exciting stuff is happening.

Not all darkness is created equal.

Are you turned on?

This is like an exercise that my sex coach, Danielle Savory, introduced to me.

Imagine that being turned on is the new normal. You get to define what "turned on" means. It can be sexual. It can be a vibe. It can be a sense of lightness.

Imagine that it is now completely acceptable to be turned on, however you define it. At work, at home, wherever you are.

Being turned on is the highest level that everyone aspires to be.

Are you there? Then imagine:

What does it look like to be a turned on being? How do they wake up? How does their hair look? How do they feel as they walk to their car and drive to their destination? How do they move through the world?

If you have had a chance to answer these questions, you have already begun to rewire your brain. Your brain is already creating new neural pathways to be that turned-on being.

Notice any sensations in your body? That is your body receiving the transmissions from your brain as it processes the questions and tries to answer them.

The more you practice being turned on and being in your brain and in your body, the more you change your brain and body chemistry. Are you feeling more alive?

That's you. You're finally coming home.

Standard of behavior

Are you really being unkind or odd or "too much," or are you following the standards of behavior set by people who don't look like you, don't know you, and don't know the first thing about the culture you are most familiar with?

I remember in Korea, my grandmother used to ignore my no's and keep feeding me food as her own way of showing me love in a scarce, post-war era. During an internship in the United States, I asked a supervisor if they wanted cupcakes, and they said no, but I gave it to them anyway thinking I was doing the right thing.

They stopped talking to me as much afterward. And did not respond to my request for a letter of recommendation. My "brand" of kindness may not have felt like kindness to that supervisor at the time.

Also in Korea, many people like to make small talk and point out obvious things like, "Are you cooking?" To someone who is literally cooking as a way of showing interest and care.

Just a few years ago at a conference, a couple of folks were running a booth, and they had some swag on the table. I picked up a notebook and said, "Oh cool, is this a notebook?" They responded, "No, it's a basketball." And then they laughed at me to imply that my question was dumb. I couldn't help but notice my face turning red.

Nobody is wrong here. We just don't know enough about each other.

We are still living in a world where we focus on the dominant culture as the "correct" culture, whether it's by nationality, race, neurotypicality, medical condition, class, or some otherwise privileged status.

Define words like "professional," "nice," and "cultured" in terms of the "correct" culture. Your existence cannot be wrong. You are not "too much" or "not enough."

They just don't know enough of your unique expansiveness, and their lack of knowledge should not be on you.

You are your own standard, and that is the only appropriate standard for you.

Which means it is impossible to violate your standard because your existence alone is the new standard.

The good girl living inside of you

If there is a good girl living inside of you wanting to please others and hate the idea of disappointing them, give her some love instead of trying to fix her or get rid of her.

You may want to forcibly and physically remove her from this world because you cannot mentally get rid of her from your mind. But the reality is that you cannot remove just her out of your body, so there may come a time when you want to erase your entire body because of her.

Before it comes to that, please consider practicing having her back so that when you feel the most vulnerable, you will be the first to say, "No, you actually deserve to be here."

You are the last person she wants to disappoint because you are her home. She has nowhere else to go. And if she is not welcome even in her own home, she will want to erase herself and take the rest of you with her because she cannot leave on her own.

So, take care of her.

Just as you would for your best friend, be there for her all night long and hold her hand. Don't toss her into the back burner and bring her out only when you are in therapy or coaching as if she is some troubled child that you cannot handle on your own.

Be there for her, one on one, and don't go anywhere as if to run from her. Because she will still be there, behind the scenes, slowly wanting to erase herself more and more as you continue to ignore her. Except she cannot be erased on her own because she is a part of you.

And when you hold her hand, there is no need to arrive at a certain place like a peaceful or a joyful place. There is no solution to arrive at. No improvement to be had. That may mean that you sometimes let her wander. Let your own mind wander. It may mean letting yourself feel drowsy. Letting her be in her quiet. Hold space for both you and her because you both are going through a lot in your one body.

And when you realize you are feeling tired, allow yourself to rest. Sometimes, not all the information we need comes to us at the same time or at the time that we want. Trust that whatever you experienced while being present with her, however long it was, was the exact experience your soul was asking for. Be willing to be incomplete. Be willing to come back for it. That is how big you are. Everything that you are is unfathomably big, including the good girl.

P.S.: The first draft of this section was written as I was processing a suicidal ideation. I used the pronoun "she/her" because I felt closest to that as I was writing it.

The function of
the good girl

Your inner good girl wants to keep the peace, not make too much of a fuss, and just do what they say. We have been told that keeping yourself small is the safest way to exist in this world.

Throughout the course of history, many women have died speaking up or doing anything that was outside of what they were told to do.

So, the good girl is keeping you safe.

When you notice yourself feeling trapped by the good girl, that is you beginning to create your own safety by questioning the status quo of what it means to be safe.

We want to thank the good girl for everything she has done. Our gratitude can coexist with the deep fire within us to create our own standards of safety.

Coaching and therapy are only a fraction of the work

Therapy and coaching have transformed and saved lives, including mine.

At the same time, therapy and coaching can also feel lonely and incomplete because the professionals may come with all kinds of useful tools and strategies that others have taught them, but they may come up empty when it comes to having sat through the darkness on their own to come to their own conclusions. This doesn't mean they have not gone through tough times.

I am talking about actually dropping everything to focus 100% on the darkness of those times without distracting ourselves, running away from it, or otherwise keeping ourselves busy to forget the darkness.

And this is not to shame the running because sometimes, it is truly fucking painful to sit in the darkness. Try sitting in actual darkness, like in the middle of a haunted house. Nobody wants to do that.

But even the mental health industry is still at its infancy when it comes to being fluent in darkness. In a world where we hyper-fetishize certifications and degrees and political correctness, what we see on paper is more valuable than what we cannot see on paper. We have been trained to find safety in what we can physically see, not in what we can feel. As a result, we often step into processing thoughts and feelings according to methods and standards set by others, and we come out of those experiences feeling disappointed, unseen, and dissatisfied.

Change on this front of the mental health industry begins with the very fundamental step of unshaming feelings. Too often we demonize feelings. We often experience a shameful feeling no matter what the original feeling is. When we feel joy, we also feel guilt. When we feel bad, we feel bad.

Instead of believing that feelings are incompatible with humanity, we must believe that feelings are the bedrock of humanity. Our feelings inform us. Sustain us. Keep us alive.

When you notice a feeling, notice the knee jerk desire to run from it. Stay with the feeling as long as you can bear it. Whether it's 3 seconds or 3 minutes. Next time, extend that time a little more.

Ask how it feels in your knees. Your heart. Throughout your body. Is it hot or cold? When you are available for it, ask questions about the sensory experience of darkness.

That is how you become fluent in darkness. Practice feeling any feeling until you are no longer afraid of it because you know exactly how to handle it.

Your feelings are not a sin

We live in a world where feelings are unprofessional: We are focused on how to do our job better and how to be more effective, and how to feel better in order to be effective. The result is always about output and results in our work.

Whether we are feeling darkness or excitement or joy, feelings in and of themselves are considered incompatible with professionalism. This is where we are deeply mistaken.

The more we attach our value to our output, the more we open ourselves to feelings that we don't want. By ignoring our feelings, we end up gaining more feelings that we are not fluent at processing.

The more we tend to the feelings that come up, the less space we will have for attachment to our output. That then yields less of the overwhelming feelings.

Your feelings are information about your direction. The professional world wants to stifle your feelings because removing information about who you really are, what you are actually capable of, and where you can go keeps you suppressed under their power.

This is not about leaving your job or starting a radical new project, though of course it can certainly include those things. But it is more about how you use the information your emotions offer. If you feel a stiffness in your neck and a pang of loneliness in your heart every time you show up to work or a relationship, for example, those sensations are offering information about how your experiences with the circumstances are stifling your truth.

This is why we want to honor our emotions exactly how they are, where they are. They are a portal to downloading our truth.

The more darkness, the better

We don't have to go around searching for darkness because it will always find us in unexpected ways.

We would not be so afraid every time it visited if we felt like we were skilled at feeling the darkness.

So, whenever the darkness visits you, you are building a skill. Here are some questions to ask when you are greeted with this opportunity:

- What is the way I want to experience this darkness right now? Sitting in it? Closing my eyes? Letting my thoughts wander? All of the above?
- What does it look like to have zero expectations out of this experience?
- If there was no right amount of time to sit in this darkness, how do I want to experience it right this second?

Or you don't have to ask any questions at all.

Whatever the case, you are building muscle. The more you lean into it, the better the workout session.

Imagination

Sometimes, we fall into a reality that we never intended. We fall into a profession that never felt right. Relationships that were meant to last just a few months last a lifetime. A single night turns into a pregnancy.

We fall into realities that turn out to be unbearable but inescapable.

(Technically we can escape it, but the consequences of escaping it feel more like a nightmare than the current reality.)

And sometimes we find ourselves fantasizing an alternate reality. Even when we are holding our child, we fantasize about the freedom we had before we had children. I certainly do.

When you do, let's stop making ourselves wrong for it. Take a comfortable stretch of time and energy to stay in that fantasy. There are days when I lie down and block out 30 minutes to just fantasize and notice where I am making myself guilty.

Let your imagination run wild. You have the freedom to think whatever you want to think. Use that freedom and see where it takes you.

Many times, as soon as you let the imagination run, you start getting bored with your imagination because it's not as fascinating as it was when you were not allowed to imagine. Because we love going after things we cannot have.

Even when we go down the road of imagining the other side of the grass, if we go down far enough, we start seeing just how much of our current reality we will need to discard to have the greener grass. Go as far as you'd like because the farther you go, the more perspective you'll get.

Other times, we get in touch with our grief over not having the life or situation we thought we would have. That grief is another part of the darkness that we get to process. Another skill-building, muscle-building exercise in being present in the darkness.

And in that grief, you may find that the fantasy you're imagining is the reality you really want right now. You may realize this the first time you imagine it or the hundredth time you imagine it. Or you might realize it the first time but see it even more viscerally each time. Or you might not, which leads you to believe that the fantasy is what you truly desire. What if we trusted that the answer would come to us at the right time?

There is no wrong outcome of imagination. There is no part of your imagination that you need to feel guilty about. Watch that fantasy play out like it's a movie.

But don't let me tell you what you will go through. It's your own psychedelic experience. Be entertained. Be curious.

Remember, you are on an adventure.

"Don't compare yourself to other people"

Not comparing yourself to other people is impossible.

Comparing is a feature of survival. Sometimes, you want the bigger slab of meat. Sometimes, you want the smaller one.

It is not the comparison that is problematic. It is the story that follows the comparison.

Is the bigger slab of meat better than the smaller one? Not for people who want the smaller one.

The stories we have in our minds about what circumstances make which person better is what is problematic.

Replace the word "better" with a specific quality. More experienced. Less pink. More clear. Less skilled.

If you understand yourself to be less skilled in a specific area, you know what to do to be more skilled.

It is not possible for someone to be "better" than anyone as a whole being. It's like saying a frog is better than a duck. It is just not something that computes because they are simply different.

Comparison must result in information, not an invasion of your humanity.

Paradox

Here's a paradox: it is very difficult to know what comes to you so easily.

We don't consciously think about how easy it is to ride a bike as an able-bodied adult.

How easy it is to answer a legal question you've been answering for decades.

How easy it is to see things the way you see them.

Because it comes to us so easily, we don't give ourselves enough credit.

You know this in your brain, but you refuse to embody it.

Embodying your excellence means allowing your body to feel it.

How does your body need to feel it?

Maybe you can say it out loud. Or think about it. Or write about it.

And when you feel the thrill and joy of excellence flowing through your system, watch how it affects the way you show up.

Parents

You do not have to force yourself to be grateful for your parents when you actually feel something else.

Our relationship with our parents does not have to be an all-or-nothing situation where we are either totally in love with them or we just cannot stand them.

If you are either, that is fine. And if you are both, that is fine, too.

What is most important is what feels true to you right now. Is it a messy combination of so many different thoughts and feelings?

If so, are you trying to organize that mess or try to figure out what is going on?

Those are symptoms of shaming. You are telling yourself that what you are experiencing needs to be "figured out." The only things that need to be figured out are problems.

You are not a problem.

You are feeling messy about your parents because you've had every variety of experiences with them. In order to "feel better" about your relationship with them, you must first honor where you are right now. If you cannot honor where you are right now, you will find it much more difficult to honor where you are wherever you go.

The reason you are here, feeling resistant to how you feel about them, after all these years, is that you have been resisting how you feel.

Stop boycotting your truth.

When you do, you may find it easier to love your parents because you will have finally learned to love yourself in your own messy truth of the moment.

You are not too much

Are you over questioning or were you taught to just blindly accept what's there?

Are you over sharing, or were you taught to hide certain parts of yourself?

Are you overthinking, or were you taught to have only certain kinds of thoughts?

Are you overpowering, or were you taught to keep your fullness small?

Are you overworking, or were you taught to work in a particular manner, frequency, and length?

If you are overwhelming other people, they just need a bigger cup to hold you. Kind of like we would never tell the ocean it is overwhelming. It simply is majestic as it is.

Everything is a tool

Everything is a tool to be more of who you are.

Your career, business, money, relationships, health—everything.

Most of the time, we have it backwards. We think we, ourselves, are the tools needed to get more out of our business and career and everything.

That is why we are endlessly using ourselves like an actual tool, attaching its value to its usefulness.

We are not a tool. We are human beings.

Use your career to see where you are skillful.

Use your business to speak the truth.

Use your money to see what you care about.

Use your relationships to witness how you love.

That is when everything starts feeling like an adventure and less like a problem.

Boredom

Boredom happens when we reject and shame the entertainment of our own imagination.

Imagine mouthing off to your idiot boss.

Imagine living on an island sipping a mojito.

Imagine having sex with the person you're not supposed to have sex with.

Once you start allowing yourself to imagine, being alone with your thoughts is not so boring anymore.

Logical vs. magical

Entertain these two thoughts:

"Making a logical decision really turns me on."

"Making a magical decision really turns me on."

Which sentence do you feel in your body more profoundly or intensely?

It can come in the form of a rush through your system, a feeling of excitement, or a thumping in your chest. But these are just symptoms. How you experience these symptoms is key.

Because sometimes we experience fear, and that fear can be a manifestation of our aliveness, or it can be a signal that the body wants to connect with the nervous system before she decides.

Listen very closely. What is your body telling you?

If you are resisting this exercise, that's okay. That is just your internal programming telling you that this is stupid because you have been taught to ignore your body.

If you were to really step into answering this question, what is your body telling you?

Logical or magical? Or both?

Each bit of tension, the flutter, the rush: it is all you. It is the language of your body.

The more you listen, the more you become fluent.

Why we worry

Worrying is one of the effective forms of distraction from what you are feeling right now.

It happens whether you are feeling great or feeling bad.

We were made to believe that all our feelings are some sort of vulnerability, so we self-teach all kinds of ways to get away from feeling as much as possible.

Worrying is one of them. It is so effective at getting us away from our feelings that it almost feels productive.

That is why we keep coming back to it over and over again. It feels like we are doing something about the uncomfortable feeling to make it go away.

Little do we know that the one way to "make it go away" is to transmute them into fuel by experiencing it. Being present with it. Kind of the way you can't shoo away the storm. Gotta sit through it with an umbrella and a margarita.

So grab a chair and feel the rain on your forehead.

Allow yourself to experience joy. Allow yourself to experience the sadness.

When you can be present no matter what you experience, there will be nothing left to worry about.

Ignorance

You do not have to let other people's ignorance become a burden for you to dismantle.

Whatever they say that arises out of ignorance (*i.e.*, not knowing your fullness) should not be an additional problem for you to address.

Instead, it is information that was transmitted to you for a very specific purpose: for you to craft your own approach to what you care about.

The ignorance stirred something in you. It probably made you angry. Toss and turn late at night. Pace around in frustration. Let it take up space in your brain.

All of these are symptoms of alchemy. You have the unique power to brew a potion that only you can create as a result of having processed the kind of ignorance that was brought to you.

If it were said to someone else without the alchemizing power you hold, that ignorance probably would have been a fart in the wind for them.

But it came to you.

You might be mad at yourself for not having addressed it right then and there. You may be upset with the fact that you "let this get to you."

Oh, honey. Let it get to you. All the way.

The messy experience you experience and the voice you craft as a result of it is the antidote for so much of the other ignorance in the world.

If the antidote was so easy to craft, there wouldn't be so much ignorance to behold.

Celebrate yourself. You have been chosen to be the magic that disempowers more ignorance in the world.

Allow your body to alchemize the experience so it can arrive at the information you're looking for on how to approach the things and people you care about.

The horse and the unicorn

We sometimes find ourselves say something like, "Well, that person does something similar to me, so I wouldn't really add much to the discussion."

That's like a unicorn saying, "Well, that horse is very similar to me, so I wouldn't really add much to the discussion."

Don't let your brain lie to you. You're a fucking unicorn.

Creativity

You are never lacking in creativity.

You were born creative, and then you were silenced.

How do you reclaim that part of you that was silenced?

Refuse to be silenced. Because your creativity is always talking to you.

You know that it's your creativity speaking whenever your brain wants to tell it that it is too much or not enough.

Let your creativity speak. It's her turn to speak now.

Sustainability

Sustainability is something's capacity to last.

It has very little to do with speed. Even if your corn field grows a lot of corn quickly, you still have to slow down and take care of the soil so you can grow more corn for the following season.

When we put speed on a pedestal, it is easy to lose sight of slowing down to take care of the foundation.

You are the foundation. Whatever it is that you are creating, your ability to replicate your successes has more to do with slowing down than with speeding up.

Ask yourself: have you been planting more seeds, or have you been making the ground fertile?

If you have been planting a lot of seeds, how can you make the ground fertile?

If you have been making the ground fertile, how can you plant more seeds?

Different signposts for different people at different parts of the journey.

You are not missing anything

You are so vast that you are five dimensional. Even imagining what that looks like is difficult to wrap our minds around because it is so large and complex.

Not large and complex the way a pile of garbage is, but large and complex the way the deep, vast ocean is.

You are a mystery with endless, majestic twists and turns.

You are already such a profound piece of architecture that there is nothing outside of you that is as worthy of exploring as you are.

With any time and energy you have, let's trek through your curves and crevices.

Everything else is just not as interesting.

I should have ...

"I should have read over that email again."

"I should have said something."

"I should have been more..."

There is nothing that you should have done. Absolutely nothing.

Because everything that you have done makes you who you are.

And you are so fucking amazing right now.

(If you are cringing upon reading that last sentence, who taught you to cringe at that sentence?)

When you realize that you are the standard and you are always meeting that standard, there are no rules to follow. Just desires to follow.

"I don't know"

The biggest source of time and energy drain is not watching tv, play video games, working crazy hours, scrolling on social media, or doing nothing.

It's these three words: "I don't know."

"I don't know what I really want."

"I don't know if I should actually do this."

"I don't know how to do it."

Or even partial knowing.

"I know I want this, but I don't know when."

"I know this is the right thing, but I can't decide."

"I know what to do, but I don't know why I'm not doing it."

These three words give us permission to distract ourselves until we know the answer. That is why we find ourselves in a sea of unmade decisions because we indulge in the comfort of not knowing.

Sometimes, not knowing is not the worst thing. We love a good mystery.

But mystery turns into confusion when we intentionally avoid answers that are meant for us.

What if the answers we are avoiding are the best news? What if these are the very answers that dissolve the loneliness, the mess, and the confusion?

You deserve to know.

If you decide that you already know and the only issue is that the answer is uncomfortable, what is the real answer?

How to never meet your goals

If you are in love with your goal because you believe it is going to get rid of the most difficult-to-solve problems, you will never achieve your goal. You will never believe that you achieved your goal even when you have technically achieved it because meeting that goal will not have solved all those problems.

You will create a bigger version of that goal, hoping that meeting a bigger version of that goal will be more effective at solving those problems.

That is not making goals. That is fantasizing impossibility.
That is why we are ignoring all the difficult-to-solve problems and going straight for the goal that we think will save us from it all.

Here's how to increase your chances:

Fall in love with the difficult-to-solve problems that will come with moving toward your goals.

For example, if your goal is quitting your job, are you in love with all the problems that come with that? Why?

If you are finding yourself not moving toward those goals, chances are that you are more in love with the problems that you are carrying now.

If you cannot wait to solve the problems that come with the difficult decision or goal, you would have made it there already.

Want to meet your goals?

Be clear about which problems you would die solving.

Admit your racism

My toddler would often prefer to read books that portrayed Black people. Michelle Obama, Jackie Robinson, Martin Luther King, etc.

At first, I was worried that she was too focused on Black people because what about Asian people? What if she forgets about her heritage?

But wait a minute, would I have thought the same thing if she were into books about white people?

I would not have said she is reading too many white books if she were reading about George Washington, Walt Disney, and Eleanor Roosevelt.

When I was worried about her reading "too many" Black books, that was my internalized white supremacy and the belief that Black people and Asian people cannot take up as much space as white people.

It makes sense. It has been true historically. But history cannot take a turn if people like me continue to perpetuate it by maintaining the status quo.

I am racist.

There is no way to dismantle white supremacy until and unless we admit to our role in perpetuating it.

After recognizing my racist parenting, I will no longer be worried that my toddler loves Black books. I will celebrate that she loves Black people not because they are Black but because they are magnificent.

If she can see how one human is amazing, she will be able to see the amazingness in other human beings.

And she will learn the truth about all kinds of oppression based on skin color so that she will be quick to notice and address her own ignorance as she navigates the world. Because even if she is born without ignorance, she will still be influenced by others' ignorance as she grows up, including mine.

She is way ahead of me.

I can do everything I can to address my ignorance everywhere it shows up so I can catch up with her.

Emotional labor

Working on yourself is not just for yourself.

When you do not have the tools to regulate your emotions, you will unload that on other people.

You will have expectations of other people to make you feel better.

That is what we call demanding free emotional labor.

When you get upset that your friend did not respond to a text.

When you expect your spouse to listen to your shit when they are unavailable.

When you need your kids to behave so you can feel more at peace.

Whenever you attribute your emotions to someone else's choice, you are expecting free emotional labor from that person.

When you learn how to feel seen and heard on your own, you become infinitely resourceful in having your own back.

Of course, we are social beings, so we will want to associate with other people. But you will be able to associate with others without expectations.

And that is the purest form of relationship.

Every time we work on the relationship with ourselves, we are deeply refining our relationship with other people.

"The 'best' and the 'brightest'"

I am not interested in being the best and the brightest.

I am more interested in being the worst and the darkest.

Have you ever been loved in your best and brightest state? Probably.

It feels good. They see you shine, and they love you for it.

But somehow... it feels incomplete.

Because the best and the brightest parts of you are only a fraction of who you are.

The more complete version of you involves your worst and darkest sides, and the love feels more complete when they see all of it and love you for it all.

When I fully own the worst and the darkest parts of myself, the parts that I want to avoid, that is when I know that whatever love I receive from that point on is the love I deserve.

Of course, the most important love is the one from myself.

That is why I am most interested in meeting my worst and darkest parts. Because when I can love myself after meeting those parts, I know that love for myself will be the true love I deserve.

That is when I will feel safe in any love that I receive, or lack thereof, because I will know that there is nothing else I can offer you to make you love me.

Lean into your worst and darkest self.

Question of the day
... and every day

If I were doing everything right, what do I want to be curious about?

How to love yourself

Step 1: Decide that you already know how.

Step 2: Look for evidence that you already know.

Step 3: Repeat over and over again.

One of the symptoms I experience with my bipolar disorder is that I often question my ability to love.

People around me tell me that I know how to love, but that is irrelevant to the fact that I do not actually feel like I know how to love.

So I repeat the steps above over and over again. Rather than a state of being or a feeling, love is more of a practice.

Sometimes the simplest answer is the best answer.

Whatever love looks like for you, decide that you are doing it right.

Everything is an illusion

Everything is an illusion. If that is the case, that means you get to choose your own illusion.

What kind of reality would you like to hypnotize yourself into?

Because you are accountable to no one.

Read that again. If that is helpful to you, keep practicing that thought until you believe it.

How to feel safe
while taking a risk

You can't. Otherwise, it won't be called a risk.

We take risks when safety is a secondary value.

The primary value is aliveness.

If you are taking a risk, your body already knows that decision comes from the decision to feel alive.

Being alive is the literal purpose of life.

When you take risks, you are living life.

My anger

I applaud all of my accomplishments to anger. Including this book.

I went to law school because I was angry that I couldn't fix my parents' marriage.

I got my dream job because I was angry that it was unfair that everyone else seemed to have great jobs.

I started my business because I was angry that I was not making as much money as my classmates.

I treasure every expression of my anger and any other uncomfortable emotions. Not because they lead to an accomplishment, but because they propel me to take all kinds of messy action that helps me gather information about who I am and what I care about.

I don't believe in the right reasons or the wrong reasons. I just believe in my reasons, and that is always good enough for me.

What are all the ways your uncomfortable emotions generated valuable information for you?

Resentment

One of the most intense feelings I've experienced throughout my life is resentment. Resentment happens when we give others the power to dictate how we think, feel, and do. This happens when we find ourselves doing something we don't want to do because we think we should be doing it. It happens even when we entertain the idea of doing something we don't want to be doing.

The reason we find it easy to do what others want us to do is that we find that information more easily accessible than what we want to do.

We don't want to know the truth of what we really want, who we really are, and where we want to go. Because what we are afraid of more than anything is failure.

"What if what I want is actually something terrible and stupid?"

"What if I don't know how to handle who I really am?"

"What if I never get to where I really want to go?"

The reason we are afraid of failure is that we think it is a bad thing.

But good vs. bad is also a construct. We never have to subscribe to constructs that aren't helpful.

Here's an alternative question to "What if I fail?": What if I aim to fail?

What if I decide to fail my way to knowing exactly what I am all about?

Here's how we get there: We remain faithful to expressing exactly what is going on with us at this moment.

If we want silence, we take up space for silence.

If we want to be angry, we take up space to express our anger.

If we notice our hands trembling with fear, we don't shame our trembling hands. We witness them.

Whenever we have to pretend or lie about our truth and suppress ourselves from expressing our truth is when resentment grows bigger.

Let's stop lying about our hands trembling with fear. Or our minds being occupied with anger.

And let's be okay that sometimes, our expression of ourselves won't always be the most tasteful or the most pleasant experience for others because it's just not possible to be pleasing to everybody.

Which do we want to pursue: attempting to do the impossible task of pleasing others or practicing our truth that agonizes to be expressed?

Because the truth is, your truth will keep coming to you because it wants to be expressed.

Whether it's in the form of boundaries, rejection, or silence, let's express what feels the truest to us in the moment.

And be okay with disappointing others. What's even more painful will be disappointing yourself.

It's the only path to kicking resentment to the curb.

Impossible to fail

Here's how to create a fail-proof system: Aim to fail.

If you are afraid to disappoint, make disappointing others the goal.

If you are afraid to feel sad, make being sad the goal.

If you are afraid to ask stupid questions, make asking stupid questions the goal.

If you are afraid to lose your job, make it your goal to feel comfortable losing anything.

When you get comfortable with the exact thing you are avoiding, it is impossible to fail.

Because you will finally have realized that it's hard to be attached to anything when you know how to handle anything.

The universe will go, "Holy shit, I can't faze this person with anything. I guess they finally realized how powerful they are."

Are you broken?

If you feel broken, as much as I want to honor the gross feelings you may be experiencing, I also want to congratulate you.

Because what's going on right now is that you are in the midst of crafting your own signature method of living life as you.

If you feel broken because you are "taking too long," you are rebelling against the idea that there is such a thing as "too long." Instead, you are setting a new paradigm that whatever time you take to do things is the exact time that is necessary to do that thing.

If you feel broken because you "cannot get this annoying thing out of your head," you are rebelling against the idea that there is such a thing as "an appropriate amount of time to think about things." Instead, you are setting a new paradigm that humans are deeply emotional and sensitive beings who actually give a shit.

If you feel broken because you "have no idea what you are doing," you are rebelling against the idea that life is nothing but a fucking blueprint. Instead, you are reminding humanity that blueprints are for buildings, not human beings.

Thank you for being broken. It makes the rest of us feel like being broken doesn't have to feel so broken anymore.

Enough shame

We have enough shame, guilt, and judgment in the world.

We don't need to add any more of it when you're trying to decide whether the email you sent was good enough.

You'll know soon enough that it destroyed nothing.

Rest vs. productivity

There is nothing that feels more productive than not resting.

There is nothing more productive than resting.

Definition of rest

Rest is the act of removing distractions from the present moment.

Rest is what happens when you disengage from movement or activity that feels like a departure from what you are truly experiencing in the moment.

If you are truly experiencing exhaustion, anything that removes you from experiencing that exhaustion is a distraction. That can be in the form of pushing yourself to keep working. That can be in the form of sitting in silence telling yourself you're an idiot for "resting."

And distractions tend to suppress and inflate. Meaning, it suppresses the exhaustion, and the exhaustion comes back tenfold.

Resting means honoring the truest thought or feeling of the moment.

When you practice being present, you are cultivating the skill to remove distractions that are not fertilizing what you are engaged with at the moment.

If you are unable to be present for your exhaustion, it will be similarly hard to be present for the more generative feelings like readiness and excitement.

When those who are skilled at rest feel ready to take on work, they have the capacity to remain faithful to that readiness instead of forcing themselves to take a break when they don't really want to, or otherwise distract themselves from the readiness.

That is why rest is the highest form of productivity. You produce the highest quality of work when you are faithful to the truest state of where you are.

When it's hard to rest

It's hard to rest when you literally cannot find the time or space for the thoughts and feelings you are experiencing.

Like, you really want to unwind after a long day, but babies are crying in the background.

Or you really want to get some work done, and an emergency comes up.

Here is a menu of sentences you can choose from that may be helpful:

1. This is fucking hard. I am not going to compare myself to other people who have it harder than I do. I am not going to minimize my hard. My hard is legitimate, and it is real.
2. Look at me, handling this steaming pile of garbage. Holy shit, I can handle things.
3. I am capable of claiming my time and space for rest, and I trust myself to be able to find the opportunity to claim it.

Also, you can create your own menu of sentences. Inspired by one of my coaches, Serena Hicks, I call the menu my spell book.

Because one of my favorite sentences is "I create my own magic on my own terms."

Happy spellcasting.

What is real?

Everything you experience is real. The pit in your stomach, the dryness in your throat in response to "what should feel mundane" is real.

There is nothing to fix or improve. Your experience is real and you are not overreacting or underreacting. You are just reacting.

If you want to feel differently or are looking for feedback on how to feel differently, it's like trying to stop yourself from sneezing. Your feelings are part of the human experience just as much as sneezing is.

If you want to transmute any of these experiences into information, the fastest way to do that is through curiosity and presence. Curiosity about what you're experiencing. Present with what is going on without judgment. (Which is, by the way, how listening works.)

And sometimes, you don't need to be present or curious at all. Kind of the way we don't need to be present and curious about our sneezes. Sometimes it happens, and we don't need to investigate every damned thing. Whatever you want goes.

The truth about compassion

I don't believe in this idea that you "need to cultivate more compassion."

You are already a compassionate human being. That is in your DNA. When you see something that moves your heart, you will want to do something about it.

We all just have different DNA and programming, and we are moved by different things. We respond differently to our own sense of compassion.

Not everyone is going to feel the exact same amount of compassion and react the exact same way to a stray puppy.

Of course, it would be beneficial for all of us to rescue a stray puppy. But here's my theory: The reason we don't express our truest sense of compassion for more things is that we assign a lot of shame to the way we harbor compassion.

When we notice something "off" at work, like someone making a condescending remark to a colleague, our first instinct is to show compassion for the colleague and do something about it. But instead, we've been conditioned to ignore that instinct and "weigh our options." We start wondering:

Am I overreacting? Am I being too much? What if I say something, and that hurts my career?

Here's the real question: What if you were willing to express every bit of your compassion exactly the way you felt?

What if you knew that your compassion, exactly as it is, is medicinal? Not as much energy would be spent suppressing and controlling your inherent compassion.

Your compassion would feel more like a free, living, breathing being.

You would be less available for rudeness, condescension, or mistreatment.

We do not need to "cultivate more compassion" for people who are assaulting our humanity.

No, I am not going to "have more compassion" for those who are treating me as sub-human. Maybe they have their own shit they're dealing with; but right now I am going to express the compassion I have for myself and draw a fucking boundary because the compassion I have for myself feels the truest to me right now.

You are compassionate already. It's time to own it.

Infinite opportunities

If you believed that there are infinite opportunities available to you, how would you show up differently?

If you trusted that you are discerning about what you want and don't want, you may even start looking forward to disappointing as many wrong people as possible to find as many right people as possible.

One right person is worth disappointing 10 wrong people.

When is the last time you entertained the idea that you are deserving of the perfect fit?

Let that thought rest and melt all throughout your body. Notice how it feels through your veins.

Perhaps that idea feels right at home. It is exactly where it should be. Because it's true.

High-quality sex

If you don't feel like you are experiencing a sufficient amount of high-quality sex but want to, I have a question for you: When was the last time you claimed high quality sex as something you love and deserve?

I want you to claim your own personal pleasure as a priority.

Not because it's productive or helpful or good. Just because you fucking declared it.

May you never let anyone else dictate the terms of how you experience pleasure in this life.

Pleasure is important, period.

What "high-quality" sex really is about

High-quality sex is not just about sex. It's about declaring pleasure as a priority. If sex is not how you experience pleasure, so be it. Most days, I don't turn to sex for pleasure.

And that is why I experience high-quality sex: because I remain true to what I desire, however I may be able to meet that desire.

When you find yourself feeling pressured or forced into doing something, that is not pleasure. When I notice myself feeling guilt for not being sexually available, I notice that sex is not a reflection of my true desire at the moment.

Then I say, "Thanks, guilt!" It just offered me information about what I want and don't want.

And if my decisions affect my partner, we are able to handle it. Together and separately. Because we trust our own and each other's capacity to handle feelings.

That's how you find exquisite pleasure: knowing what you want and not making yourself wrong for it.

The real reason for consistency

The real reason behind consistency is that consistently showing up every chance you get to communicate the sentences you generate in your mind—whether it's for a presentation or an email or a text or a post—it takes a lot of tries to find words that feel like home.

Consistency is never about other people.

It is about you. And expanding your capacity to express yourself.

The question is NOT "are you consistently showing up for your people?" Because when that is the question, we start becoming performative because we keep feeling the need to guess what other people want.

The real question is: Are you consistently showing up for yourself and deciding each day that what you are experiencing is worth expressing?

This includes silence. Are you also deciding that showing up for yourself can look like not sharing anything at all?

Because showing up for your own silence is harder than actioning your way through performative consistency. In your silence, you actually have to sit with the uncomfortable thoughts and feelings that stare you in the face because there is no other noise to distract you.

And confronting who you are and where you are is the scariest and hardest thing because we're more familiar with performing.

True consistency is not about taking action. It is about being willing to witness yourself so that you continue to build capacity for expressing your truth in its rawest form.

True consistency is about being consistently you.

"I think"

I've been taught at several points in my life that I should write with more certainty by removing words that indicate uncertainty, like "I think."

So instead of "I think that was not the best purchase," I should say, "That was not the best purchase."

That made sense to me for a while.

But I have grown to fall in love with uncertainty.

We don't need to be certain with everything in our lives. There is a sense of curiosity and possibility that comes with wonder and humility in place of certainty.

And certainty is something that can be nurtured and nourished through wonder and humility. Having wonder and humility about a thought allows us to entertain different sentences to see which ones feel most true to us.

When we play with the different sentences and find what feels right, we arrive at actual certainty because we draw ourselves closer to the words that feel truest to us in the moment.

That is why I now have no problem saying "I think" before I say what's on my mind because that is the truth of what I am experiencing. It is something I am not declaring with absolute certainty, but there is a sense of magic in what I am thinking.

What have you been taught to suppress, regardless of how inconsequential it may seem?

It may not be so inconsequential after all.

The truth about my marriage

I got married for the "wrong" reasons. I was 25 and ambitious when I got married. This is what my life's checklist looked like at the time:

1. Get married.
2. Make money.
3. Be successful (whatever the fuck that means).

I thought, if I get 1 out of the way, then I can focus on the other 2 because I really need to make money and I can't waste time fucking around with romance.

When I met Daniel, I thought he was a reasonable enough person to marry. My aunt was friends with his family, so chances were low that he would swindle me out of my money and success. Also, it was pretty apparent that he really liked me.

My decision to get married, in and of itself, was a stress response. I inherited the cultural norm that it is most acceptable to get married, have kids, and be successful regardless of what I really wanted to do. I was very much subscribed to such expectations because I was hell-bent on pleasing everyone and getting approval from everybody (and their dog).

And, of course, the unmet need for constant approval manifested itself throughout our marriage. I required Daniel to always be available for me, even when he needed space. I required him to become a cookie cutter version of what I wanted in a husband so that I could feel prouder of myself.

There was no love in sight, at least on my part. I kept throwing out the idea of divorce because it was embarrassing that I didn't know how to love. And there was a deep-cutting slice of me that wanted to take this marriage to the edge so that I could prove that I was right all along—that I was never going to be good enough for anybody.

On the one hand, I was desperate to prove that I was good enough. On the other hand, I wanted to just rip the bandage off and come to terms with the fact that I was never going to be good enough.

I was the embodiment of incongruence: not knowing who I was or where I was going.

But even when I had no idea what was going on in my life, and everything was burning down, Daniel somehow remained certain in his love for me.

Even when you don't have the slightest clue about the value of your own existence, your lovability is inevitable.

Even when you are absolutely and actively trying to make every creature on this planet not like you, you will remain lovable.

The fact that you are lovable can show itself in different ways: in the form of staying in a marriage to remain dedicated to one channel of lovability, leaving a marriage for a heightened sense of lovability elsewhere, never getting married to redefine what lovability looks like for you, or getting married multiple times to keep experimenting with how you want to engage with the truth of your lovability.

There is no right or wrong way your lovability manifests itself. It simply is.

The way you experience the truth of your lovability will be messy. It may even be hurtful to you and other people. It may take some time to arrive at a place that feels most like home.

But none of this is in conflict with your lovability. In fact, it is part of building your own manifestation of what your flavor of lovability looks like for you.

When I witnessed my lovability in the form of Daniel's steadfast commitment to me, I accepted that as my conduit to learn how to love. Sometimes I learned by imitating. Sometimes by listening. Sometimes by being comfortable with being wrong.

People learn how to love at different times in their lives in different methods with different people. Love is the unpredictable magic and mystery of humanity. There is no definition that does the word much justice.

And all that effort you are putting in, the willingness to experience it all, the messy mix of feelings you experience, that just may be what love is.

Because your existence, in and of itself, is lovable, perhaps everything you are and everything you do is the most pure form of love there is.

"Why isn't it working?"

Sometimes we find an approach that works for a particular instance, and so we think we should keep using that approach. And when it doesn't work again in what appears to be the exact same circumstances, it's confusing.

Kind of like chewing gum for nausea in one instance when it doesn't necessarily work in a later instance.

Or approaching someone today with what we think is the same kind of compassion we approached them with yesterday, yet it fails to elicit the same response.

Or the same systems that worked in your business last year don't work again this year.

When this happens, we begin looking for external factors like the weather or the economic state of the world.

But here's a simpler and truer explanation: While we are the same person, we are always in a different place. Where we were yesterday in our house is a different place from where we are today in the exact same house and even the exact same square footage.

The variable? Time.

Time is a measure of location.

Even two breaths ago, you were in a different place. Now, you are in a place with one more sentence than you were one sentence ago.

Time is a measure of location because of the things that take place with time. Every breath and every sentence you take in is like decoration for the universe that you are in. The universe that is unique to you.

With every second, your universe is evolving. Explosions are afoot, a star is fading, and a new planet is being formed. All of this happens along the trajectory of time.

The bad news might be that what worked yesterday doesn't work today.

But the good news is that life is not a thing to be worked but to be explored.

I would rather choose exploring the universe than working the universe.

If you weren't looking for solutions for your universe but were exploring the vastness of your universe, what would you find?

Why we feel overwhelmed

Do you ever think the following: Ugh, it's just one thing after another over and over again. I am never going to be able to overcome the overwhelm.

The reason we feel like everything is coming at us, and it feels like we are drowning, is that we did not use the prior instances of overwhelm to build capacity for overwhelm.

Let's say Overwhelming Event 1 happens on Wednesday. Then Overwhelming Event 2 happens on Thursday. Then Overwhelming Event 3 happens on Friday. If we have not built our capacity to process Overwhelming Events 1 and 2 before Friday comes around, then we are going to feel an overload in our system by the time we have experienced all three events without having processed any of them at all.

Of course, we are not always going to have the perfect opportunity and timeline to process the overwhelming thoughts, feelings, and circumstances that come around.

But there will be a time where you get to choose whether you are going to take some space to process it or to ignore it.

When you decide to do the hard work of processing each overwhelming event, gather some tools to process them, and be willing to experiment to find what works and what doesn't. You will become more fluent at handling overwhelming events of greater frequency and size.

The reality is that we have become quite attached to overwhelm; while it makes us feel stuck, it also gives us permission to avoid doing something about it because the solution appears to be absent and impossible.

Some people mistake the numbing of their sense of overwhelm with processing and building capacity for overwhelm; and when this happens, people eventually break.

Either way, our bodies will tell us what to do. Our bodies will give us the information we need.

None of this is instructive as much as it is informative. And sometimes information is helpful, while other times we choose to ignore that information.

If you find this information helpful, how will you choose to confront overwhelm and when?

Being an Asian woman

Being Asian and being a woman are not necessarily the first two descriptors that I would use for myself, but such is the case for others when they see me, and that shapes the way I interact with others.

In some ways, being an Asian woman has been an honor. There is no reason or explanation for it. If not for the socialization that being an Asian woman is a disadvantage, it's simply a privilege to be exactly the way I am.

And in some ways, being an Asian woman has been a bitch.

I worry about things I don't want to worry about that are specific to that descriptor. These are actual questions I have asked myself both consciously and subconsciously:

1. What would I need to do to look as skinny and as pretty as all the other Koreans I grew up with?
2. What would I need to do to meet both Korean standards and American standards of being a woman?

3. What would I need to do to be taken seriously by white men in the U.S. so that I can advance my place in the world?

4. What parts of me do I need to suppress and erase to appear acceptable to other Americans?

5. How can I look and act to please the most powerful and leveraged class, race, and community of people in the U.S.?

6. In what ways do I need to be more Asian and more feminine to please even more people?

7. How can I be better than all the other Asians I am competing with for white approval?

These questions affect my actions. These questions perpetuate white supremacy and the patriarchy—and probably some other harmful hierarchical construct that I am not even aware of.

It's pretty fucked up when I have not only been harmed by the systems in place while also weaponizing those systems to perpetuate power imbalances.

I am both the victim and the perpetrator.

It sucks ass.

Being in this position has yielded a lot of insight, curiosity, and progress.

Yet sometimes, I just need to sit down and marinate in the suck. Because there are some things in life that just suck, and I won't dare dishonor it by trying to wiggle my way out of it.

Burning those bridges

At some point in my life, I started getting tired of preserving bridges.

I noticed that I was erasing my humanity in the process. I was performing for others, lying about how I really felt, and pretending to be someone I was not. I was done with it.

I no longer cared about how "powerful" the other person was or how much they could "benefit" my future.

I decided that I was going to be my own bridge to everything. I was willing to get comfortable getting rejected more often, having to build my own credibility, and being misunderstood.

Anything else began feeling like a steaming pile of waste.

What feels like a steaming pile of waste to you?

You don't have to get rid of it right now or address it somehow right now.

But I want you to ask yourself how your body is reacting to what's going on. Collect information.

Once you have enough information, you will feel compelled to take action.

On your terms. No one else's.

My greatest shame

A few weeks after my first child turned one, I placed a boiling pot of ramen on a place mat on the kitchen table. As I stepped into the kitchen to get some water, she pulled off the place mat and sustained second degree burns on her arms and face.

I have been grappling with the shame since then. I have ripped myself apart. I've had a long-standing fight with the feeling of grief.

I had been on a journey to get rid of this shame. Until I decided I am no longer available to get rid of that shame.

That shame is part of me. I WILL tell myself that I am really fucked up and that I am not good enough for my children.

Because that is my truth. And I own it.

I will not let anyone take that away from me.

But the surprising thing is, after I made this decision, I started showing up more fully for my kids.

Why? Because I stopped denying the parts of myself that I felt uncomfortable with.

Maybe one day I will be totally unashamed of my mistakes when it comes to parenting. I just know that it is not happening at the moment.

Paradoxically, that is how I get to be an example of what is possible for my kids. I won't be able to erase the pain and the scars my child had to experience. But I will always be available for her when she experiences shame as she ventures out into the world.

She will at least know what it feels like to know that someone has her back in the heaviest end of darkness.

What is your greatest shame? How is it the very thing you won't let anyone take away from you?

How to trust yourself

Do you distrust yourself?

Maybe it's too scary. It's terrifying.

Trust that.

Trusting yourself is about trusting the information that your body offers to you.

If your body is terrified, treat it like anybody else.

What would you do for a terrified person?

You would probably give that person a hug.

You would probably not rush them.

The only reason we have trouble trusting ourselves and what our bodies are trying to tell us is that we are in a rush for answers.

The answer is already there.

Your body is telling you. Be present with her.

That is the answer at this very moment.

Printed in Great Britain
by Amazon

23557141R00159